BRITISH LOCOMOTIVE CLASSES

PRC

PRINCIPAL 'BIG FOUR' LOCOMOTIVE CLASSES AS AT 1945

INTRODUCTION

Towards the end of World War 2 in Europe, the Locomotive Publishing Co (acquired by Ian Allan Ltd in 1957) greeted the new era somewhat uncharacteristically. The company's well-known address of 3 Amen Corner, in the shadow of St Paul's Cathedral, had been destroyed in a bombing raid during 1940 and the move had been made to 88 Horseferry Road, London SW1. From this address in the late spring of 1945 *Modern Locomotive Classes* was published, despite the prevailing shortage of paper.

For the reasonable price of six shillings (30p) the new title, under the authorship of the authoritative (and under-rated) technical writer, Brian Reed, provided a useful semi-technical guide to British railways' steam motive power before Nationalisation, and in advance of some familiar early postwar locomotive designs. Notably missing from *Modern Locomotive Classes* are the SR Bulleid Light Pacifics, GWR 'Counties', LNER 'L1' 2-6-4Ts and the LMSR Ivatt 2-6-0s of both types, and 2-6-2Ts. One has the suspicion that the late Brian Reed was no admirer of Edward Thompson's works as one or two of the more controversial rebuilds of earlier locomotive classes are missing when other contemporary literature tended to give them the limelight.

The Introduction of the 1945 Edition comments that 'certain classes described in these pages originated over a score of years ago, but the designs have been largely followed for engines built during the intervening years and are still the most up-to-date of their type'. This is fair comment but it is interesting to note how relatively aged some of these designs were: for instance, the Fowler '4F' 0-6-0 (1911), Gresley 0-6-2T (1920) and Churchward '43XX' 2-6-0 (1911). Engines of each of these classes continued to serve our railways well into the 1960s.

Nearly 60 locomotive designs are featured in this book which in this new edition has been re-titled to *British Locomotive Classes 1945*. The figure conflicts with the apparent total of 61 descriptions because of the separate inclusion of rebuilt examples and Gresley 'A1' as well as 'A3' which can hardly be regarded as different designs. It is not a facsimile of the 1945 Edition as the publishers have aimed to improve reproduction as compared with a 'dot for dot' treatment of the half-tones as originally printed. The majority of prints have been matched, although in one or two cases an alternative view taken at the same time has been used.

Michael Harris
January 1991

© LPC 1945

First published 1945 by Ian Allan Ltd

This edition published 1996 by the Promotional Reprint Company Ltd, Kiln House, 210 New Kings Road, London SW6 4NZ exclusively for Bookmart Limited, Desford Road, Enderby, Leicester LE9 5AD

ISBN 1 85648 342 8

Printed and bound in China

4-6-2 STREAMLINED LOCOMOTIVE, L.M.S.R.

IN 1937 five streamlined Pacific engines were built at Crewe to work the then new Coronation Scot train between London and Glasgow; subsequently others were constructed for hauling the principal London-Scotland and London-Merseyside passenger trains, and were named in the Duchess and City series. In wheelbase, boiler, and general particulars they are similar to the non-streamlined Duchess class, but owing mainly to the aerodynamical shroud the engine weight is about three tons greater. City class streamliners have been built since war began.

The boiler is the same as that of the latest non-streamlined Pacifics. Its diameter tapers top and bottom over the back ring from 5 ft. 10 in. to 6 ft. 5½ in. outside, and the distance between tube-plates is 19 ft. 3 in. The front ring is parallel and has an outside diameter of 5 ft. 8⅝ in. The barrel contains 129 tubes of 2⅜ in. o.d. by 11 s.w.g. and 40 flues of 5¼ in. o.d. by 7 s.w.g., which provide an aggregate heating surface of 2,577 sq. ft. The firebox, with combustion chamber, gives 230 sq. ft. towards the total evaporative surface of 2,807 sq. ft. The flues contain 1 in. elements of 11 s.w.g. thickness, and which are trifurcated to give three elements in parallel forward and three in parallel backward, and produce a superheating surface of 856 sq. ft. The grate area is 50 sq. ft. The boiler shell is of nickel steel and the inner firebox of copper with Monel metal side stays in the outer, top, and throat plate rows, and steel stays elsewhere. Live and exhaust steam injectors with 13 mm. cones feed the boiler, and deliver the water through top-feed clackboxes and trays set on the front ring of the barrel. The pressure of 250 lb. per sq. in. is limited by four 2½ in. Ross pop safety valves, and the boiler is equipped with a sand gun so that the tubes can be cleaned in the course of a long run.

Four 16½ in. by 28 in. cylinders have divided drive over the first two pairs of coupled wheels; they have 9 in. piston valves with six narrow rings, given a maximum travel of 7 in. by two outside sets of Walschaerts gear. Ball and roller bearings are fitted to all the valve motion joints. Coupling and connecting rods are of nickel-chrome steel, and 50 per cent. of the reciprocating weights are balanced, this being more or less L.M.S.R. standard practice for new main-line passenger engines. The coupled axleboxes are steel castings with pressed-in brasses having whitemetal on the bearing surface. The load on the bogie is transmitted through side bearers and not through the centre plate. All the laminated bearing springs for the engine and tender are of silico-manganese steel.

At 75 per cent. of the working pressure the tractive effort at the rims of the 6 ft. 9 in. wheels is 35,250 lb., which gives a factor of adhesion of 4.25 when related to the 67.1 tons on the coupled wheels. The engine weight is 108.1 tons and that of the 4,000 gal. tender 56.35 tons, giving a total of 164.45 tons for the engine and tender together.

4-6-2 EXPRESS LOCOMOTIVE, L.M.S.R.

IN 1933, under the direction of Mr. W. A. (now Sir Wm.) Stanier, the L.M.S.R. put into service its first two Pacific locomotives, No. 6200 *The Princess Royal*, and 6201 *Princess Elizabeth*. Ten further engines were built at Crewe works in 1935 and embodied several important modifications, principal among which were the enlarged firebox with combustion chamber, and the doubling of the number of superheater elements. The grate area is the same, and also the general mechanical details, but the first part of this description refers to the 1935 batch, Nos. 6203-6212, and to Nos. 6200-1 as now running. The missing number, 6202, is borne by the turbine locomotive.

The boiler is tapered uniformly from 6 ft. 3 in. outside at the back to 5 ft. 8⅝ in. at the front, and on both sides. The barrel contains 112 steel tubes of 2¾ in. o.d. by 11 s.w.g. and 32 flues of 5⅛ in. o.d. by 7 s.w.g., which together give a heating surface of 2,167 sq. ft. The firebox has a heating surface of 217 sq. ft., and the total evaporative surface is thus 2,384 sq. ft. The superheater incorporates the bifurcated type of element, and has a total surface of 623 sq. ft. The Belpaire wide firebox has a grate area of 45 sq. ft. and the combustion chamber is about 3 ft. 3 in. long. Water is fed to the boiler by live and exhaust steam injectors delivering through a series of feed trays. No steam dome was fitted originally, and steam was collected by a pipe upturned above the firebox tubeplate, but domes are being fitted now just behind the top feed clackbox. The barrel plates are of 2 per cent. nickel steel.

Four 16¼ in. by 28 in. cylinders are provided, the inner pair driving the first coupled axle and the outer pair the second coupled axle. Four sets of Walschaerts gear are used, and give the 8 in. piston valves a maximum travel of 7¼ in. Ball and/or roller bearings are provided at the joint pins. With 75 per cent. of the boiler pressure of 250 lb. per sq. in. the tractive effort is 35,250 lb., giving a factor of adhesion of 4.25. The six-wheeled tenders carry 4,000 gal. of water and 10 tons of coal, and weigh 54.65 tons when full; the engine plus tender total is 159.15 tons.

Some years later further unstreamlined engines of the Duchess class were set to work, and the illustrations on this page refer to them. Compared with the earlier engines, the distance between the leading and centre coupled wheels has been reduced by 9 in. and the wheel diameter increased by 3 in.; the cylinders are ¼ in. larger and rearranged, and the exhaust steam passages are now more direct; and the outside connecting rods are longer. The boiler now is 6 ft. 5½ in. dia.; pitched 9 ft. 6 in. above the rails; it contains 129 tubes of 2¾ in. o.d. and 40 flues of 5⅛ in. o.d., 19 ft. 3 in. long. The tube and flue heating surface is 2,577 sq. ft., the firebox surface 230 sq. ft., and the evaporative total 2,807 sq. ft. The triple 1 in. superheater elements give a surface of 856 sq. ft.; the grate area is 50 sq. ft. or 11 per cent. more than in the origina L.M.S.R. Pacifics. Eventually, all the L.M.S.R. Pacifics, streamlined and otherwise, will have the same boiler type. Unstreamlined Pacifics named in the City class were still being built in 1944.

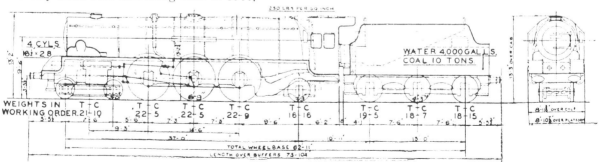

4-6-2 TURBINE LOCOMOTIVE, L.M.S.R.

THE joint product of the L.M.S.R. Crewe Works and the Metropolitan-Vickers Electrical Co. Ltd., the Turbomotive, No. 6202, was completed in 1935, and subsequent to lengthy experiments has been working on the Euston-Liverpool route. The wheel arrangement and numerous mechanical parts are similar to those of the two original Pacifics built in 1933, but later reboilering has brought Turbomotive more into line with the standard Pacific.

No condenser is incorporated, and this means a considerable simplification in design at the expense of reduced theoretical thermal efficiency. There are two turbines at the front of the locomotive, one for forward drive and the other for backward running. The main, or forward, turbine is located on the left hand side and has a shaft horsepower of 2,000 when using steam at 250 lb. pressure and with a temperature of 750 deg. F. The torque is transmitted to the leading coupled wheel through a treble reduction gear of the double helical type which is permanently in mesh, and when the reverse turbine is in operation the steam supply to the forward machine is cut off, and the blades idle in the opposite direction. The final wheel of the transmission incorporates a form of individual axle drive which prevents shocks from the rail being transmitted to the turbines. The wheels are 6 ft. 6 in. in dia., the same as the first Pacifics of the L.M.S.R., but 3 in. less than those of the Duchess and streamlined varieties.

From the smokebox tubeplate backwards the boiler-firebox unit was a duplicate of that on the 1935-built Pacifics, and provided a total heating surface of 2,167 sq. ft., a grate area of 45 sq. ft., and a superheating surface of 577 sq. ft. As no condenser is fitted, the turbine exhaust can be turned up the chimney and used to provide draught for the fire, but owing to the low pressure an automatically-variable double blast pipe has been found necessary. In addition to the normal high thermal efficiency of the turbine when worked at constant load and speed, No. 6202 has a further aid to low steam consumption in that the carriage heating steam is bled from the turbine exhaust. Steam enters the turbine through six nozzles, which are opened and closed one by one from a control box in the cab.

As there are no reciprocating parts, and thus no hammer blow, an axle load of 23.3 tons has been permitted. Timken roller bearings are fitted throughout the engine and tender. The engine scales 110.55 tons, and is thus the heaviest tender locomotive in Britain, since the rebuild of *Cock o' the North*. The tender is of the standard L.M.S.R. 4,000 gallon type (except for the roller bearings) and its weight brings the total engine and tender weight up to 165.2 tons. In 1944, Turbomotive, after being in Crewe works with a damaged turbine and transmission, emerged with a new boiler. Smoke deflector plates have been fitted at the side of the smokebox since 1939.

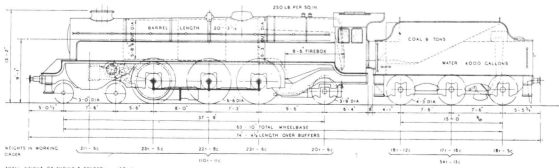

4-6-0 ROYAL SCOT LOCOMOTIVE, L.M.S.R.

A TREMENDOUS advance in the express locomotive practice of the L.M.S.R. was made in 1927 by the introduction of the 50 three-cylinder Royal Scot engines built by the North British Locomotive Co., Ltd. Previously the biggest express engines had been the *ex* L. & Y. 4-cylinder 4-6-0's, the L.N.W. four-cylinder "Claughtons", and the Caledonian two-cylinder 4-6-0's, all of which were pre-1914/18 designs. The Royal Scots were designed to eliminate as far as possible the then frequent double-heading up Shap, and their normal unpiloted load over the summit is 450 tons. Later, another 20 engines to the same design were constructed at the Derby works of the L.M.S.R. The smoke deflector plates were not fitted originally. To clear the loading gauge the whistle is projected horizontally in front of the cab.

The parallel boiler has a maximum internal diameter of 5 ft. 7⅜ in. and the barrel is 14 ft. long with a distance between tubeplates of 14 ft. 6 in. The Belpaire firebox is not fitted with a combustion chamber but the throat plate and tubeplate are inclined forward to give increased firebox volume. The grate, with an area of 31.2 sq. ft., is fitted with a drop section. There are 180 tubes of 2 in. o.d. and 27 flues of 5⅛ in. o.d., which gave a heating surface of 1,892 sq. ft. The total evaporative surface of 2,081 sq. ft. is made up by the addition of 189 sq. ft. from the firebox. The designed working pressure was 250 lb., but for some years no effort has been made to keep the figure above 220 lb. or so in actual service. A superheating surface of 445 sq. ft. is provided by the 27 elements of 1¾ in. o.d., but the latest type of superheater with the same number and diameter of elements gives only 399 sq. ft.

Divided drive from the 18 in. by 26 in. cylinders was adopted, the inside cylinder driving the leading built-up balanced crank axle, and the outer pair the second coupled axle through 11 ft. 3 in. connecting rods of 50/60-ton Vibrac steel. Three independent sets of Walschaerts gear drive the 9-in. piston valves. At 75 per cent. of the boiler pressure, assuming 250 lb., the tractive effort is 29,200 lb., giving a factor of adhesion of 4.8 against the 62.5 tons resting on the coupled wheels. The total engine weight is 84.9 tons, and 127.6 tons with the standard 3,500-gal. tender. A steam brake, giving a retarding force of 43 tons, actuates blocks on the coupled wheels, and further cylinders apply blocks on the bogie and tender wheels. 4,000 gal. tenders weighing 54.65 tons are now fitted, and bring the engine plus tender weight up to 139½ tons.

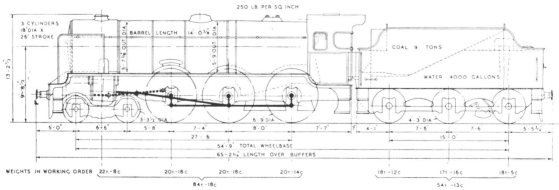

4-6-0 REBUILT ROYAL SCOT LOCOMOTIVE, L.M.S.R.

ALMOST coincidentally with the rebuilding of the first of the Stanier class 5XP three-cylinder 4-6-0 engines early in 1943, attention was turned to the fitting of the same type of boiler and exhaust arrangements to the Royal Scot 4-6-0 class, so that eventually the whole 183 engines of these two classes will have standard and interchangeable taper boilers. Authority was given in 1943 for 20 Royal Scot conversions to be undertaken at Crewe as engines came in for new boilers and cylinders, and No. 6103 *Royal Scots Fusilier* was the first to be dealt with. It is understood that the rebuilds are to be known as the Converted Royal Scot class, but will retain the original power classification of 6P. Actually, there is one further engine which may be regarded as a rebuilt Royal Scot, with a taper boiler having 1,988 sq. ft. of heating surface and 392 sq. ft. of superheating surface; that is the engine *Silver Jubilee*, which is fitted with a Kylchap double exhaust system.

The taper boiler now replacing the original parallel boiler has a tube heating surface of 1,667 sq. ft., a firebox heating surface of 195 sq. ft., a total evaporative surface of 1,862 sq. ft., a grate area of 31.2 sq. ft., and a superheating surface of 357 sq. ft. Further boiler details will be found in the description of the rebuilt 5XP locomotives. Compared with the unrebuilt Royal Scot boiler, the evaporative heating surface is more than 200 sq. ft. less, the firebox heating surface is 6 sq. ft. greater, the grate area is the same, the superheating surface is 42 sq. ft. less, and the working pressure remains at 250 lb. per sq. in. The appearance is improved by fitting a smokebox flush with the barrel.

Three cylinders 18 in. by 26 in. are retained, but are to a modified design; as before, the outside ones drive the centre pair of 6 ft. 9 in. coupled wheels and the inside cylinder drives the front coupled axle. As in the new 5XP engines, there is a double blast pipe and chimney, and a partitioned smokebox. The original wheelbase dimensions have not been changed, but the maximum axle load has been reduced by nearly half a ton, and the adhesion weight is now 61 tons in place of 62.5 tons previously. The total locomotive weight is almost two tons less at 83 tons, and the load carried on the bogie also is a little less than in the original design. No change has been made in the standard 4,000 gal. six-wheel tender.

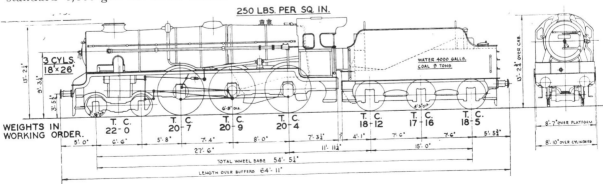

4-6-0 5XP LOCOMOTIVE, L.M.S.R.

IN 1934 Mr. W. A. Stanier introduced the first of the 5X class three-cylinder 4-6-0 engines for express passenger traffic, and 113 of these engines were built at Crewe and Derby, and by the North British Locomotive Co. Ltd. Experience in traffic working showed it to be desirable to increase the superheating and firebox heating surface, and the latest engines embody these and sundry other modifications, and are classed "5XP". The class is widely spread south of Glasgow, and operates on the Western, Midland and Caledonian Divisions.

A dome has been fitted to the taper boilers and the top feed is taken through a clack box just in front. The boiler barrel is 12 ft. 10 in. long and tapers from 5 ft. $8\frac{3}{4}$ in. at the back to 5 ft. at the front; it contains 159 tubes of $1\frac{7}{8}$ in. o.d. by 11 s.w.g., and 24 flues of $5\frac{1}{8}$ in. o.d. by 7 s.w.g. arranged in three rows. The length between tubeplates is 13 ft. 3 in., and the evaporative surface provided by tubes and flues is 1,460 sq. ft.; the firebox surface is 181 sq. ft., and the total evaporative surface 1,641 sq. ft. The Belpaire firebox has an outside length of 10 ft. and a grate area of 31 sq. ft. The superheating surface provided by the elements of $1\frac{1}{4}$ in. o.d. by 11 s.w.g. is 307 sq. ft., an increase of 35 per cent. compared with the original 5X engines, and the regulator has been taken from the superheater header and is now located in the dome. These engines are now all scheduled for rebuilding with new boilers and double chimneys, and their characteristics and appearance in this guise are as given on page 7.

All three 17 in. by 26 in. cylinders have separate sets of Walschaerts gear giving a travel in excess of 6 in. to the piston valves. The drive is divided, the inside cylinder being located well forward and driving the front single-throw crank axle, and the outside pair driving on to crank-pins in the centre pair of coupled wheels. At 75 per cent. of the boiler pressure of 225 lb. per sq. in. the tractive effort is 23,500 lb., giving a factor of adhesion of 5.7 against the 60 tons resting on the coupled wheels. The total engine weight is 79.55 tons in working order and 73.25 tons light, these figures being a slight reduction compared with those of the 5X engines. Tenders of both the 3,500 and 4,000 gallon standard types were fitted to the first 113 engines of class 5X, but the new 5XP locomotives have the 4,000 gallon pattern, which weigh 27.8 tons empty and 54.65 tons full. The maximum working order weight of engine and tender thus is 134.2 tons. Several interesting trials have been made with engines of this class to check exactly the performance and the fuel and water consumptions, particularly on the Midland Division.

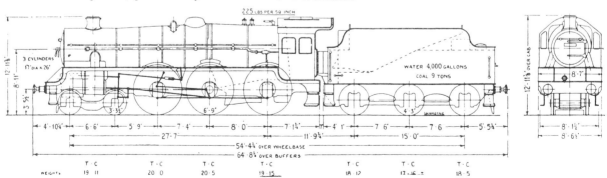

REBUILT 5XP 4-6-0 LOCOMOTIVE, L.M.S.R.

THE ENGINES of the Stanier three-cylinder 4-6-0 5XP class were reboiled and given larger super-heaters comparatively soon after their construction in 1934-35, and other detail changes have since been made. Early in 1943 two engines, *Phoenix* and *Comet*, were provided with entirely new taper boilers and exhaust arrangements, and this modification is to be applied to the rest of the class as they come in for overhaul or new boilers. On reboiling, the power classification is raised to 6P, the same as the Royal Scot class. The principal chassis alterations are a rear extension of the frames and a new smokebox saddle.

As now running, the latest versions have a boiler barrel tapering from 5 ft. 5 in. at the front to 5 ft. $10\frac{1}{2}$ in. at the back in a length of 12 ft. 11 in. There are 198 tubes of $1\frac{3}{4}$ in. o.d. and 12 s.w.g. thick, and 28 flues of $5\frac{1}{8}$ in. o.d. by 7 s.w.g. thick. Tubes and flues have a heating surface of 1,667 sq. ft., and the Belpaire firebox 195 sq. ft., giving an evaporative total of 1,862 sq. ft. The grate area is 31.2 sq. ft., the working pressure 250 lb. per sq. in., and the superheating surface (from $1\frac{1}{4}$ in. elements) 357 sq. ft., all these being small increases over the previous standard figures. The new boiler (class 2A) is pitched with its centre 9 ft. $3\frac{1}{4}$ in. above rail level, and detail modifications to it include new top-feed clackboxes on the front ring of the barrel instead of on the dome side. The original 5XP engines of 1934-35 had domeless boilers. The firebox is 10 ft. 3 in. long, the same as the original and rebuilt Royal Scot locomotives.

The three cylinders at 17 in. by 26 in. and the divided drive to the 6 ft. 9 in. coupled wheels remain as before. The piston valves are controlled by the usual form of Walschaerts gear. But the steam is now exhausted to the atmosphere through a double blast pipe and chimney, following experiments in improving the steaming qualities of express locomotives in general on the L.M.S.R. The adhesion weight, compared with the earlier 5XP engines, is increased by $1\frac{1}{2}$ tons to 61.5 tons; the engine weight is now 82 tons and that of the tender 53.65 tons, giving a combined total of 135.65 tons. The bogie is of the pattern standard for L.M.S.R. locomotives of the 4-6-0 wheel arrangement and has 3 ft. $3\frac{1}{2}$ in. wheels spread over a base of 6 ft. 6 in. The tender itself is notable for the large coal capacity—for a 4-6-0 engine—of 9 tons.

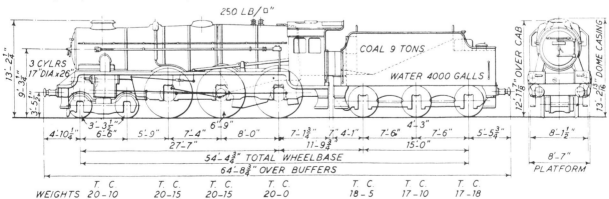

4-6-0 PATRIOT CLASS LOCOMOTIVE, L.M.S.R.

THE Baby Scots originated in an extensive rebuild of two of the old L.N.W.R. Claughton class 4-6-0 engines, so extensive, indeed, as to produce virtually new locomotives. A total of 42 engines was "converted" and another ten were built new at Crewe in 1934. These engines are not considered quite the equal of the Royal Scots, and are classed as 5XP, that is, the same as the Stanier three-cylinder 4-6-0 class. At one time they worked a good deal of the express passenger traffic on the Midland division, and more recently have been operating on the Euston-Birmingham two-hour services. The design incorporates the external appearance of the Royal Scots, but with a slightly longer chimney, smaller boiler and firebox, and a 3,500 gal. tender, and is often known as the Patriot class after the name carried by No. 5500. These engines are fast runners, and have been timed at 93 m.p.h.; in performance they have been little inferior to the unrebuilt Royal Scots.

The parallel domed boiler has a maximum external diameter of 5 ft. $5\frac{1}{8}$ in. and contains 140 tubes of $2\frac{1}{8}$ in. o.d. and 24 flues of $5\frac{1}{4}$ in. o.d., which together contribute 1,552 sq. ft. to the evaporative total of 1,735 sq. ft. The remaining 183 sq. ft. is made up by the Belpaire firebox, which is 9 ft. 6 in. long outside and has a grate area of 30.5 sq. ft. The working pressure is 200 lb. per sq. in. and is limited by two Ross pop safety valves. As with the Royal Scots, the whistle projects horizontally through the front of the cab, but in this case the reason is one of standardisation of mountings rather than restrictions of height. The superheater has a surface of 365 sq. ft. from $1\frac{1}{2}$ in. elements.

The three 18 in. by 26 in. cylinders have piston valves driven by independent sets of Walschaerts motion. The inside cylinder drives the leading coupled axle. At 75 per cent. of the working pressure the tractive effort at the rims of the 6 ft. 9 in. wheels is 23,500 lb., giving a factor of adhesion of 5.7 against the 59.75 tons resting on the coupled wheels. The engine weight is 80.75 tons—$4\frac{1}{4}$ tons less than that of the Royal Scots. The 3,500 gal. tenders carry $5\frac{1}{2}$ tons of coal and weigh only 42.7 tons, giving an engine plus tender weight of 123.45 tons.

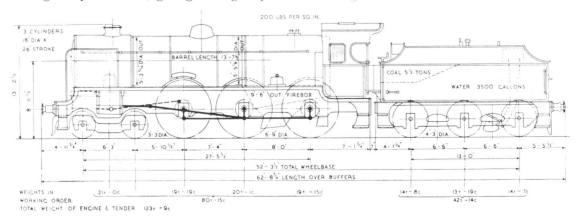

4-6-0 MIXED TRAFFIC LOCOMOTIVE, L.M.S.R.

AS with the three-cylinder express engines, the first two-cylinder 4-6-0's with 6 ft. wheels were built with low temperature superheaters and smokebox regulators. They were given the designation class 5, and were built at Crewe and by the Vulcan Foundry and Armstrong Whitworth. A modified version, classified 5P5F is now being introduced, and its design incorporates similar modifications to those detailed for the three-cylinder express engines. Although styled generally mixed-traffic locomotives, classes 5 and 5P5F are used extensively on express passenger trains on the Western, Midland, and Scottish sections. As with the 5XP three-cylinder engine, several boiler designs have been used since the introduction of the class.

In front of the firebox tubeplate the boiler is the same as that of the 5XP express engines, and contains 159 steel tubes of $1\frac{7}{8}$ in. o.d. and 24 flues of $5\frac{1}{8}$ in. o.d. which together give a heating surface of 1,460 sq. ft. The Belpaire firebox, however, is shorter by 9 in., and gives a heating surface of 171 sq. ft. in conjunction with a grate area of 28.6 sq. ft. Housed in the flues are 24 elements $1\frac{1}{4}$ in. o.d. by 11 s.w.g. which give a superheating surface of 307 sq. ft. The boiler is fed through the usual top feed apparatus by live and exhaust steam injectors. New boilers have 151 tubes of $1\frac{7}{8}$ in. o.d. and 28 flues of $5\frac{1}{8}$ in. which give a surface of 1,479 sq. ft. The firebox surface is 171 sq. ft., the evaporative surface 1,650 sq. ft., the superheater surface 359 sq. ft., and the grate area, as before, 28.6 sq. ft.

At 75 per cent. of the boiler pressure of 225 lb. per sq. in. the two $18\frac{1}{2}$ in. by 28 in. cylinders produce a tractive effort of 22,450 lb., giving a ratio of 5.3 to the adhesion weight of 53.15 tons. By reason of the relatively low maximum axle load of 17.9 tons and a commensurate hammer blow, these engines can work over the great majority of L.M.S.R. routes and have done good work on such sections as the ex-Highland division. In full working order the 5P5F locomotives weigh 70.6 tons, and in the empty condition 64.1 tons, both values being slight reductions on the weights of the original class 5 machines. Tenders of 4,000 gallons capacity are fitted to the latest engines, as well as to the earlier batches, and are provided with the latest anti-splash water pick-up apparatus. They are standard with those fitted to various 4-6-0 express classes.

Careful and extensive balancing and running tests have been undertaken with these engines, and have resulted in 50 per cent. of the reciprocating weights being balanced. With 66 per cent. balanced, tests showed that the driving wheels rose $2\frac{1}{4}$ in. from the rails at an equivalent speed of 104 m.p.h.

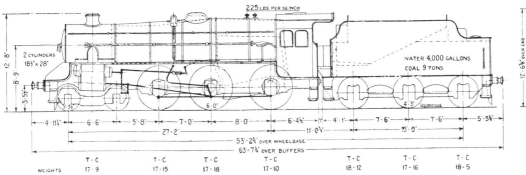

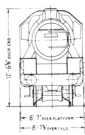

2-6-0 LOCOMOTIVE, L.M.S.R.

WHEN, in 1933, further mixed traffic engines were considered necessary, a batch of 40 Moguls were put in hand at Crewe, and they were delivered in 1934. Then numbered 13245-13284, these locomotives were allocated to the Scottish, Midland, Western and Central divisions when new.

Although of the same general power as the preceding 245 engines of the 2700 (or 13000) class, the design is quite different, and embodies the now familiar characteristics of a taper boiler working at a fairly high pressure, top-feed, a low-temperature superheater, and relatively small cylinders. Originally the firebox was the same as those of the 4-6-0 mixed-traffic engines, and the boiler was similar, but shorter. It gave a tube heating surface of 1,256 sq. ft., a firebox surface of 156 sq. ft., and a grate area of 27.8 sq. ft. The present boilers taper from 5 ft. 8⅜ in. to 5 ft. in diameter in a length of 11 ft. 10 in.; they house 136 tubes of 2 in. o.d. and 21 flues of 5¼ in. o.d., which give a heating surface of 1,216 sq. ft. The firebox contributes 155 sq. ft. to the total evaporative surface of 1,371 sq. ft.; and the 21 elements of 1⅛ in. o.d. give a superheating surface of 224 sq. ft. compared with 193 sq. ft. in the original boilers. The grate area remains at 27.8 sq. ft.

The two outside cylinders are 18 in. by 28 in., the reduction of 3 in. in the diameter compared with the 2700 class being possible owing to the higher working pressure of 225 lb. per sq. in. The smaller diameter also has permitted the cylinders to be arranged horizontally. The 5 ft. 6 in. coupled wheels are steel castings with tyre retaining rings of the Gibson pattern, and the balance weights are built up of steel plates on each side of the spokes, with lead filling between. These details are more or less standard for new L.M.S.R. locomotives. The coupled axleboxes are of steel with pressed-in brasses having whitemetal pockets.

At 75 per cent. of the boiler pressure the tractive force is 23,200 lb.; the original adhesion weight being 55.5 tons, this effort gave an adhesion factor of 5.35, but the present adhesion weight is 59.5 tons and the factor 5.7. The engine weight is now 69 tons and the engine plus tender weight 111.3 tons, compared with 65 and 107.2 tons originally. The design of the pony truck is different from that of the Hughes-Fowler Moguls; the weight is taken through side bolsters, side check springs are fitted to give smoother running, and the wheels are unbraked. Steam brakes operate blocks on the coupled and tender wheels, and vacuum brake apparatus is incorporated for applying the train brakes. The vacuum pump for the train brakes is worked off the left-hand crosshead, and is prominent in the illustration above.

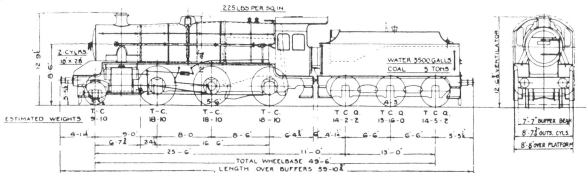

0-6-0 GOODS LOCOMOTIVE, L.M.S.R.

THE standard 0-6-0 engines which work so much passenger and goods traffic on the L.M.S.R. originated with Sir Henry Fowler's 3835 class on the Midland Railway about the 1914-18 era, and with sundry modifications the design has been used for new construction since. It is simply a classic example of the classic British 0-6-0 engine. There are over 750 in service, of which Nos. 3835-4026 were built by the Midland before grouping.

The boiler incorporates the usual Midland Belpaire firebox with a heating surface of 123 sq. ft. and a grate area of 21 sq. ft. On top of the box are mounted two Ross pop safety valves set to blow off at 175 lb. per sq. in. The barrel is composed of two telescopic rings, $\frac{9}{16}$ in. thick, with a mean diameter of 4 ft. 8 in. and a length of 10 ft. 6 in. It contains 146 tubes of $1\frac{3}{4}$ in. o.d. and 21 flues of $5\frac{1}{8}$ in. o.d., both of steel, and 10 ft. $10\frac{1}{2}$ in. long. The tubes and flues provide a heating surface of 1,034 sq. ft., giving a total evaporative surface of 1,157 sq. ft. The superheating surface is 253 sq. ft. in some of the engines and 313 sq. ft. in others.

Cast integrally, the two inside cylinders are 20 in. dia. by 26 in. stroke, and have overhead inside admission piston valves of 8 in. dia. driven through rocking shafts by Stephenson link motion. The cylinders are inclined downwards to the driving axle at a slope of 1 in $8\frac{1}{2}$; they exhaust into a blast pipe with a nozzle of $4\frac{5}{8}$ in. dia. set $1\frac{1}{2}$ in. below the centre line of the boiler. All wheels have underhung laminated springs 3 ft. $2\frac{1}{2}$ in. long and composed of 14 plates $\frac{1}{2}$ in. thick and 5 in. wide. A steam brake is fitted to the engine and gives a retarding force of 0.157 tons per lb. pressure in the cylinders; vacuum equipment for operating the train brakes is standard.

At the rim of the 5 ft. 3 in. wheels the tractive effort at 75 per cent. of the boiler pressure is 21,600 lb., giving a factor of adhesion of 5.1 The tender is of the standard 3,500 gal. pattern.

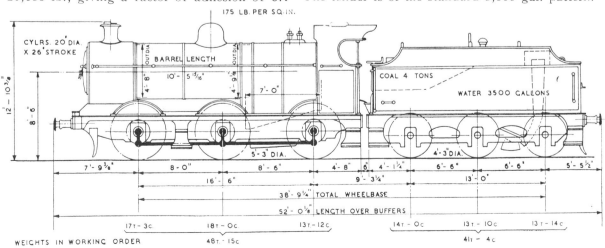

0-8-0 MINERAL LOCOMOTIVE, L.M.S.R.

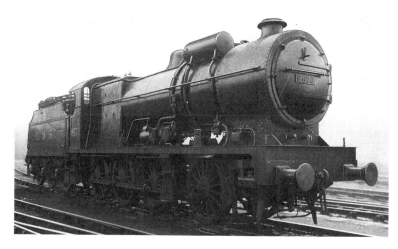

ONE hundred 0-8-0 locomotives for main-line mineral traffic were built at Crewe Works in 1929-30 and are known as the 9500 class. They were developed from the "G.2" eight-coupled engines of the *ex*-L.N.W.R., but with numerous improvements, including the substitution of two inside sets of Walschaerts gear instead of the Joy motion, 3 in. larger wheels, 20 lb. higher boiler pressure, and smaller cylinders. They are not fitted with any form of automatic brake for possible passenger train working. Three of the class were at one time equipped with A.C.F.I. feed-water heaters, and one of them so fitted is illustrated at the head of this page. The L.M.S.R. power classification is 7F. The running plate is clear of the wheels, so that no splashers are needed, but this necessitates a buffer beam rather deeper than usual.

The boiler is very similar to that of the L.N.W.R. locomotives, but the working pressure is 200 lb. and there are two pop safety valves on top of the Belpaire firebox. The tube heating surface is 1,434 sq. ft., and the firebox surface 150 sq. ft., giving an evaporative total of 1,584 sq. ft. The 5 ft. barrel contains 124 tubes 2 in. o.d. and 24 flues of 5 in. o.d. and 14 ft. 10½ in. long. The superheating surface is 352 sq. ft. and the grate area 23.5 sq. ft. The boiler is fed by one live steam and one exhaust steam injector.

The two inside 19 in. by 26 in. cylinders are inclined steeply downwards to drive the second coupled axle, and at the rims of the 4 ft. 8½ in. wheels a tractive effort of 26,300 lb. is available at 75 per cent. of the boiler pressure, and related to the engine weight of 60.75 tons gives a factor of adhesion of 5.35. The maximum axle load is 17.85 tons, borne by the second, or driving axle. The wheelbase of 18 ft. 3 in. is appreciably longer than that of other L.M.S.R. 0-8-0 and 2-8-0 locomotives. The tender weighs 41.2 tons in full working order, and the engine plus tender total is 101.95 tons. Steam brakes, raised smokeboxes, chimneys and cabs are among the Fowler details included. Steam sanding gear is fitted for use in both directions of running. No continuous brake equipment is incorporated, so that the locomotives are not suited to passenger train working, and, indeed, are seen comparatively infrequently on miscellaneous freight trains.

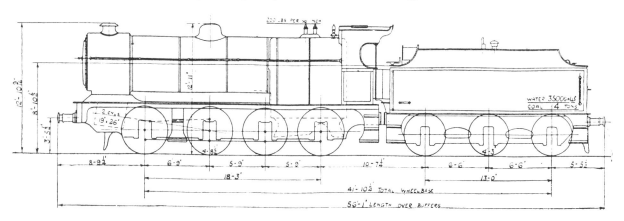

2-8-0 FREIGHT LOCOMOTIVE, L.M.S.R.

AN addition to the heavy mineral traffic engines of the L.M.S.R. was made in 1935, when 12 two-cylinder engines, Nos. 8000—8011, were turned out of Crewe Works. They were the first Consolidation engines built for the L.M.S.R., and the first modern engines of that design for any of the constituent companies, except for the Fowler locomotives on the Somerset & Dorset Railway. With a maximum axle load of merely 16 tons, the new batch has an L.M.S. power classification of 7F, and is intended for operation on all regular freight routes. Later engines have a power classification of 8F.

The taper boiler is of the domeless type and is fed by one live steam and one exhaust injector through top feed apparatus. The boiler is tapered on the top from 5 ft. outside diameter at the smokebox to 5 ft. 8⅜ in. at the firebox, in a length of 11 ft. 10 in. The original barrel contained 136 tubes of 2 in. o.d. and 11 s.w.g., and 21 flues of 5¼ in. o.d. and 7 s.w.g., both 13 ft. 3 in. long. Tubes and flues together have a heating surface of 1,308 sq. ft.; the evaporative total of 1,463 sq. ft. is made up by the addition of 155 sq. ft. from the firebox. The outside Belpaire firebox has a length of 9 ft., and the grate area is 27.8 sq. ft. The superheater has a surface of 235 sq. ft., and the header contains the regulator. Bigger boilers with an evaporative total of 1,650 sq. ft. and a grate area of 28.6 sq. ft. have since been fitted; the barrel contains 202 tubes of 1¾ in. and 21 flues of 5¼ in., giving 1,479 sq. ft. of heating surface. The superheater has a surface of 245 sq. ft. The most modern top-feed lay-out is now incorporated.

The two 18½ in. by 28 in. cylinders have piston valves with a travel of 6½ in. and actuated by Walschaerts gear. High tensile molybdenum-manganese steel is used for the connecting and coupling rods and, as usual in modern L.M.S. practice, the laminated bearing springs are of silico-manganese steel. The front Bissel truck has a radius bar 6 ft. 7¾ in. long. Hand sanding gear is fitted, and a jet of water comes into operation behind the coupled wheels when the sanding gear is in operation in order to clear the sand off the rails and prevent interference with track circuits. The engine weighs 70.5 tons of which 62 tons are available for adhesion, giving a factor of adhesion of 4.84 against the tractive effort of 28,600 lb. with 75 per cent. of the working pressure. The latest 8F engines weigh 72 tons, of which 63 tons is adhesive. The latest tenders weigh 54.65 tons.

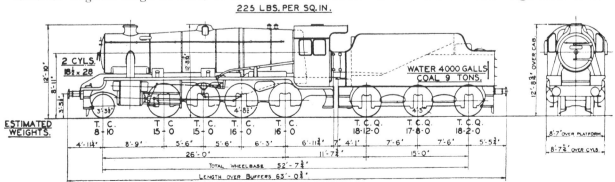

2-6-0+0-6-2 BEYER-GARRATT LOCOMOTIVE, L.M.S.R.

A TOTAL of 33 Beyer-Garratt engines of the 2-6-0+0-6-2 wheel arrangement is in service on various routes of the L.M.S.R., e.g., hauling coal trains and the returning empties between Toton sidings and Cricklewood yard, London, a distance of 126 miles. The first three of these engines were set to work in 1927, and in 1930 an order for 30 more was placed. All 33 locomotives are now fitted with Beyer Peacock's patent self-trimming rotating coal bunker, but the three 1927 locomotives originally had the ordinary type, as had some of the 1930 engines. The Beyer-Peacock bunker is in the shape of a conic frustrum and is rotated by a two-cylinder steam engine. Braking or heating equipment for passenger working is not fitted. Since construction, the operating range of these locomotives has been increased, and they work trains to York and to stations on the ex-Great Northern main line of the L.N.E.R.

It was decided to incorporate a number of standard details from the 2-6-0 mixed traffic engines, and this produced limitations both in the design and everyday performance. The boiler, with a diameter outside of 6 ft. 3 in., has an evaporative heating surface of 2,137 sq. ft. made up of firebox, 183 sq. ft.; tubes and flues 1,954 sq. ft. There are 209 tubes of 2 in. o.d. and 36 flues of 5½ in. o.d.; the length between tubeplates is 12 ft. 5 in. A surface of 500 sq. ft. is provided by the 36-element superheater and the grate area is 44.5 sq. ft. The firebox is of the Belpaire type and the working pressure is limited to 190 lb. per sq. in. by Ross pop safety valves. The outer firebox is 8 ft. 5 in. long, and has a sloping grate; it is of the simple, straightforward type permitted by the Garratt frame layout. The boiler-firebox-cab unit is supported on a rigid underframe, or cradle, pivoted at each end on the frame structures of the corresponding engine unit.

The four 18½ in. by 26 in. cylinders have overhead piston valves actuated by Walschaerts gear, and at 75 per cent. of the boiler pressure they develop a tractive effort of 40,250 lb. at the rims of the 5 ft. 3 in. coupled wheels. This gives an adhesive factor of 6.9 against the 122.1 tons resting on the two sets of coupled wheels with the locomotive carrying full supplies. Under the same conditions the total weight is 155.5 tons, and the maximum axle load 21.0 tons. The three engines built in 1927 had 116.5 tons of adhesion weight and the whole locomotive scaled 148.75 tons; the water capacity was 4,700 gal. and the coal space equivalent to 7 tons. The 1930 batch, and the first three engines since modification, carry 4,500 gal. of water and 9 tons of coal; most of the water is contained in the tank above the front engine. The overall width of these locomotives is comparatively narrow, being only 8 ft. 7 in. Water pick-up apparatus is fitted to the front engine unit, and can be used in either direction of running.

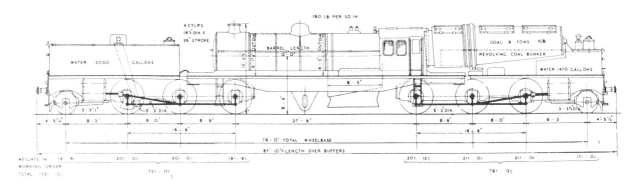

2-6-2T LOCOMOTIVE, L.M.S.R.

AS a development and improvement of the 2-6-2 tanks built during Sir Henry Fowler's regime, a series of 20 engines of the same wheel arrangement was built at Derby in 1935, the numbers being 71—90. These engines have been allocated to branch lines and suburban duties requiring a lighter machine than the standard 2-6-4 tanks, but on which an up-to-date and efficient engine was desirable.

The ubiquitous taper boiler forms the steam generating plant and within a length of 10 ft. 5¾ in. the barrel tapers from 4 ft. 9 in. at the back to 4 ft. 2 in. at the smokebox. The superheater was comprised of only seven elements of 1⅛ in. o.d. by 13 s.w.g., which gave a surface of merely 76 sq. ft. There were 135 tubes of 1¾ in. o.d. by 11 s.w.g. and 7 flues of 5⅛ in. o.d. by 7 s.w.g., which gave a heating surface of 774 sq. ft., the tube length being 10 ft. 10½ in. The Belpaire firebox, with a grate area of 17.5 sq. ft., contributed 104 sq. ft. to the total evaporative surface of 878 sq. ft. The working pressure is limited to 200 lb. by two 2½ in. pop safety valves. Certain engines had boilers giving 1,046 sq. ft. of heating surface,, including 107 sq. ft. from the firebox. After the beginning of the war, boilers tapering from 4 ft. 6 in. to 4 ft. 9 in. were fitted without increasing the locomotive weight more than 1¼ tons. The heating surface is now 996 sq. ft. from tubes and flues plus 111 sq. ft. from the firebox, making a total of 1,107 sq. ft. The new 14-element superheater provides a surface of 145 sq. ft. The illustrations on this page show the reboilered engine, which has 171 tubes of 1⅝ in. o.d. and 14 flues of 5 in. o.d., and a grate area of 19.2 sq. ft.

Long-travel piston valves controlled by Walschaerts gear are located above the 17½ in. by 26 in. cylinders, which are inclined down towards the second coupled axle. At 75 per cent. of the working pressure a tractive effort of 19,000 lb. is obtained. With an adhesion weight of 46.45 tons with tanks and bunker full, this means a factor of 5.5. The locomotive weight in full working order is 71.25 tons, but when empty this is reduced to 57.5 tons. The usual L.M.S.R. steam brake with vacuum ejector and control for the train brake is fitted, and also the standard mechanical sanding gear with hot water jet for clearing away the sand from the rails after use. The leading and trailing trucks are of the Bissel type with the weight taken through side bolsters, and with a radius bar 6 ft. 7¾ in. long. With the new boilers the weight is 72½ tons, distributed as shown below.

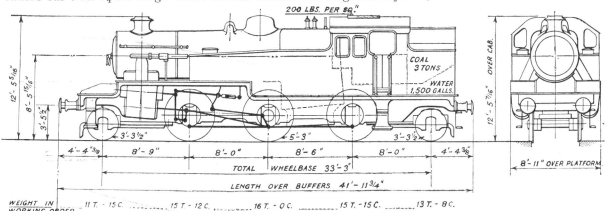

2-6-4T 3-CYL. LOCOMOTIVE, L.M.S.R.

THE first 2-6-4T engines built under Mr. Stanier's direction were turned out of Derby Works in 1934, and were 37 in number, Nos. 2500—2536. Although they have the same wheelbase dimensions, they are quite different from the 125 earlier engines of Sir Henry Fowler's design and are somewhat more powerful. The first locomotives were all sent to the London, Tilbury & Southend section, but since that time the class has been distributed more widely.

A taper boiler of different proportions to those carried by the Mogul tender engines was used. In a length of 11 ft. 10 in. it tapers from 5 ft. 3 in. outside diameter at the back to 4 ft. 9 in. at the front, and contains 145 tubes of $1\frac{3}{4}$ in. o.d. by 11 s.w.g. and 12 flues of $5\frac{1}{8}$ in. o.d. by 7 s.w.g., both types being 12 ft. 3 in. long. The evaporative heating surface is 1,147 sq. ft., made up of 1,010 sq. ft. from the tubes and flues and 137 sq. ft. from the Belpaire firebox. The grate area is 25 sq. ft., and the grate itself is fed through a standard sliding firedoor with an anti-glare screen. The 12 superheater elements of $1\frac{3}{8}$ in. o.d. and 13 s.w.g. thickness provide the very moderate superheating surface of 160 sq. ft. Two $2\frac{1}{2}$ in. pop safety valves on the firebox top are set to blow off at 200 lb. per sq. in. The present boilers have 148 tubes of $1\frac{3}{4}$ in. o.d., 18 flues of $5\frac{1}{8}$ in. o.d. and 12 ft. 3 in. long, 1,126 sq. ft. of tube heating surface, 139 sq. ft. of firebox surface, a grate area of 26.7 sq. ft. and a superheating surface of 185 sq. ft. The top feed is housed in a casing of its own, just in front of the dome.

The three 16 in. by 26 in. cylinders all drive the centre coupled axle, and three sets of Walschaerts gear are used to actuate the piston valves. Two-bar crossheads are used for the outside cylinders and a single-bar arrangement for the inside cylinder. At 75 per cent. of the boiler pressure the tractive effort is 21,700 lb., giving a factor of adhesion of 5.9 against the adhesion weight of 57 tons with tanks and bunker full. In full working order the engine weight is 92.2 tons, and when empty, 74.1 tons. The cab is completely enclosed, and has sliding side windows and drop lights in the doors. The drive is on the left-hand side, and tip-up seats are provided for the driver and fireman. The coal bunker is narrowed at the top in order to improve the lookout when running bunker first. The trailing bogie and leading truck are different to those incorporated in the earlier 2300 class, the weight being taken through the side bearers. Water pick-up apparatus is not incorporated. The hand-operated sanding gear to each side of the centre coupled wheels and to the front of the leading pair is supplemented by a water de-sander available for either direction of running. The L.M.S.R. power classification for these passenger tank locomotives, and for the others with two cylinders (see next page) is 4P.

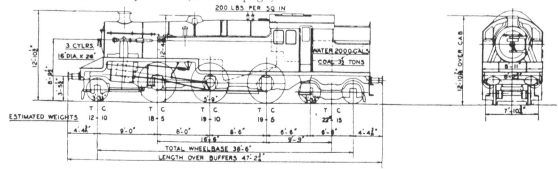

2-6-4T 2-CYL. LOCOMOTIVE, L.M.S.R.

THE 125 Fowler two-cylinder and 37 Stanier three-cylinder 2-6-4 tanks were supplemented in 1935-36 by eight further engines of the same wheel arrangement with taper boilers and two cylinders. Numbered 2537—2544, these machines were built at Derby. Although based generally on the preceding three-cylinder engines, the boiler design was modified to give an increase of 15 per cent. in the superheating surface, which, however, does not raise it above a moderate temperature superheater. The present boilers have only 8 per cent. more evaporative surface, but the superheating surface is 30 per cent. greater. Further engines have been constructed at the company's works in various batches since 1935/36, including the war years.

The original boilers had 1,168 sq. ft. of evaporative surface, and then other boilers with 1,265 sq. ft. were provided. The present boilers taper from 5 ft. 3 in. to 4 ft. 9 in. in a length of 12 ft. 2½ in.; they contain 157 tubes of 1¾ in. o.d. and 21 flues of 5⅛ in. o.d. The tube and flue surface is 1,223 sq. ft. and that of the firebox 143 sq. ft., giving a total of 1,366 sq. ft. The grate area is 26.7 sq. ft. and the superheating surface 245 sq. ft. A steam turret is fitted on top of the firebox back plate, and supplies steam to the vacuum ejector, steam brake, injectors, train heating, pressure gauges and sight feed lubricator. This arrangement is common to most of the modern L.M.S.R. locomotive types, but two details which are not among the usual standards are the two live steam injectors (in place of one live steam and one exhaust steam) and the vacuum ejector in place of the usual crosshead pump. The top feed is now located ahead of the dome, and the dome itself has been moved back towards the firebox, as may be seen by comparing the two illustrations on this page.

The two cylinders have a stroke of 26 in. and the unusual measurement of 19⅝ in. for the initial bore. The lubrication of the pistons, piston valves, and piston rod packings is effected mechanically, and also the lubrication of the coupled axleboxes. Other standard features are the use of manganese-molybdenum steel for the connecting and coupling rods, silico-manganese steel for the ribbed plates of the main bearing springs, adjustable spring hangers, cast steel axleboxes with babitted pressed-in brasses, Gibson retaining rings for the tyres, and balance weights of lead with flanking and top plates of steel.

At 75 per cent. of the boiler pressure the tractive effort is 21,800 lb., giving a factor of adhesion of 5.3 against the adhesion weight of 51.7 tons. The weight in full working order is 87.85 tons, and light, 70 tons. Earlier engines weighed 91 tons, distributed as shown on the diagram below. This class differs from the three-cylinder 2-6-4T locomotives in having water pick-up gear for use in either direction of running.

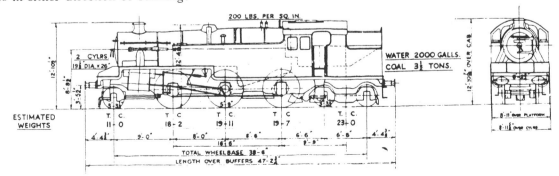

0-6-0T SHUNTING LOCOMOTIVE, L.M.S.R.

THE standard 7100 class 0-6-0 shunting tanks of the L.M.S.R. were introduced first during the regime of Mr. George Hughes, and now number some hundreds of engines built by the L.M.S.R. and various private builders. They are of a simple, straightforward non-superheated design with inside cylinders. In certain respects they may be said to be descendants of Samuel Johnson's 0-6-0T engines on the old Midland Railway. The power classification of these engines for the L.M.S.R. traffic department is 3F, the F, of course, representing "freight"; but passenger trains are worked in some districts. Seven engines were at one time in the Somerset & Dorset list; two have been converted to 5 ft. 3 in. gauge for service on the N.C.C. line.

A parallel boiler with a Belpaire firebox is used. The barrel is of 4 ft. inside diameter and houses 194 tubes of $1\frac{3}{4}$ in. o.d. 10 ft. $10\frac{3}{4}$ in. long, which give a heating surface of 967 sq. ft. The firebox heating surface is 97 sq. ft. and the evaporative total 1,064 sq. ft. The grate area is 16 sq. ft. Two Ross pop safety valves limit the working pressure to 160 lb. per sq. in. Some engines have had boilers with 196 tubes and 1,074 sq. ft. of surface. The first 50 locomotives of the Hughes regime had Ramsbottom safety valves.

The two 18 in. by 26 in. cylinders have slide valves actuated by Stephenson link motion, and assuming 75 per cent. of the boiler pressure they produce at the rims of the 4 ft. 7 in. wheels a tractive effort of 18,400 lb. The weight varies from 49.5 to 50.5 tons between the different batches, giving an adhesive factor with full tanks of 6.1, or of 5.2 with tanks empty. The tank capacity is 1,200 gal. and the bunker holds $2\frac{1}{4}$ tons of coal. Steam and hand brakes are fitted, and also vacuum apparatus for the operation of passenger train brakes. Steam sanding gear is fitted to the front and back of the driving wheels.

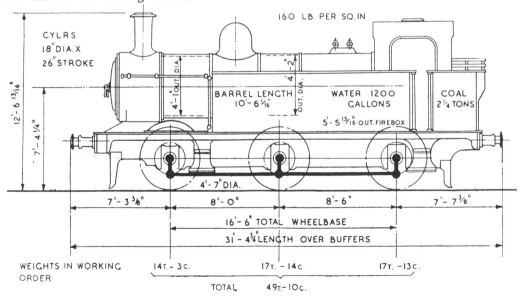

2-6-0 LOCOMOTIVE, N.C.C. (L.M.S.R.)

ALL the principal Belfast-Londonderry and Belfast-Portrush passenger trains on the 5 ft. 3 in. gauge lines of the L.M.S.R. Northern Counties Committee are now hauled by two-cylinder 2-6-0 engines with 6 ft. wheels and the moderate axle load of 17½ tons maximum. These engines, of which there are nine dating from 1933-36, three dating from 1938-40, and two dating from 1942-43, were built at Derby works and re-erected at the York Road, Belfast, shops of the N.C.C. Most of them are named. The original tenders of the first nine engines have been replaced by larger units holding 3,500 gal. of water and 7 tons of coal, and weighing 47¾ tons loaded, so that heavy trains can be hauled over the 66 miles between Belfast and Portrush without replenishment. In ordinary service these locomotives have been timed at 76-77 m.p.h., and the writer has known occasions when they were worked for several miles at cut-offs of 10 per cent. or less.

The design of these Ulster engines may be traced back to that of the Hughes-Fowler parallel-boiler 2-6-4T locomotives of the L.M.S.R. The boiler has a minimum inside diameter of 4 ft. 6⅞ in. and a length between tubeplates of 11 ft. 5 in. It contains 121 tubes of 1¾ in. o.d. and 21 flues of 5⅛ in. o.d., which give a total heating surface of 951 sq. ft.; the firebox surface is 130 sq. ft. and the evaporative total 1,081 sq. ft. The superheating surface is 266 sq. ft., the grate area 25 sq. ft., and the working pressure 200 lb. per sq. in. The Belpaire firebox is 4 ft. 4½ in. wide outside at the bottom and the inside copper box 3 ft. 8¼ in. Top feed delivery has always been embodied in the design.

The outside cylinders slope downwards sharply, and drive the centre coupled wheels. They have a diameter and stroke of 19 in. by 26 in. and the 9 in. piston valves are actuated by Walschaerts motion which gives a travel of 6¾ in. in full gear. The tractive effort at the wheel rims with 75 per cent. of the boiler pressure is 19,550 lb., which gives an adhesive factor of 5.9 against the 51½ tons carried on the coupled wheels. The 2,500-gal. 5-ton tenders of the first nine engines weighed only 33 tons when full.

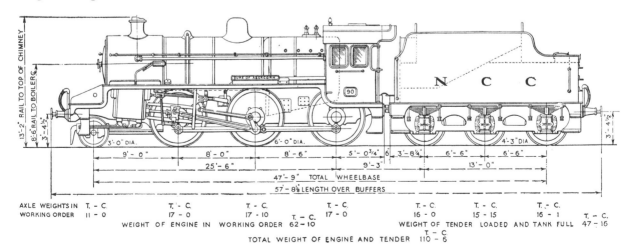

4-6-2-2 STREAMLINED LOCOMOTIVE, L.N.E.R.

PERHAPS the most powerful steam passenger locomotive now running in the British Isles is the simple-expansion rebuild of the once well-publicised four-cylinder compound water-tube boiler locomotive No. 10000 of the London & North Eastern Railway. In its present form it retains the 4-6-4—or, more strictly, 4-6-2-2—wheel arrangement, and has a firebox and cylinders similar to those of the *Cock o' the North* 2-8-2 passenger design, though the working pressure is higher. Normally, it works heavy trains on the London-Yorkshire main line of the old Great Northern Railway.

The taper boiler of the rebuild has a minimum outside diameter of 5 ft. 9¼ in. and a maximum diameter of 6 ft. 5 in.; the front ring is parallel. Within this boiler are 121 steel tubes of 2¼ in. o.d. and 10 s.w.g. thick and 43 flues of 5¼ in. o.d. and 5/32 in. thick, and 17 ft. 11¾ in. long. Including 237 sq. ft. from the firebox, the total evaporative surface is 2,598 sq. ft., the grate area is 50 sq. ft., and the boiler pressure—relieved by two 3½ in. Ross pop safety valves—is 250 lb. per sq. in. A regulator of the double-beat type leads steam through a 7 in. internal pipe to the header of a 43-element superheater, and the elements of 1½ in. o.d. provide a superheating surface of 750 sq. ft. Integral with, and behind the steam dome is a steam collector to which the steam rises through a series of ½ in. slots cut in the top of the boiler barrel. The boiler is fed by an 11 mm. live steam injector and a 12 mm. exhaust steam injector.

The three 20 in. by 26 in. cylinders are cast separately, and the exhaust from the outside cylinders is carried to the blast pipe through passages in the cast steel smokebox saddle. Exhaust is through a Kylchap double blast pipe. In addition to the revolving weights, 40 per cent. of the reciprocating weights are balanced in the 6 ft. 8 in. coupled wheels. The piston valves are operated by Walschaerts-Gresley gear arranged to give a maximum cut-off of 65 per cent. with a travel of 5¾ in. The connecting and coupling rods are of fluted section nickel-chrome steel.

Braking of the locomotive is by two 27 in. vacuum cylinders giving a maximum total braking force equivalent to 93 per cent. of the weight on the coupled wheels. Bowden wires are used for the control of the sanding gear, cylinder cocks, and whistle. Other fittings include bucket seats for the driver and fireman, Flaman speed indicator, and turbo-generator set for the electric lighting. After rebuilding in 1937, the coupled wheels and rods could be floodlit at night from the electrical installation. Against the adhesion weight of 66 tons the tractive effort of 36,500 lb. at 75 per cent. of the boiler pressure gives an adhesion factor of 4.05. The locomotive weighs 107.85 tons in working order, a value which has been exceeded in Britain only by the L.M.S.R. Turbomotive and streamlined Pacifics, and by the *Cock o' the North* as it ran originally. The corridor tender weighs 64.15 tons, and the combined engine and tender 172 tons.

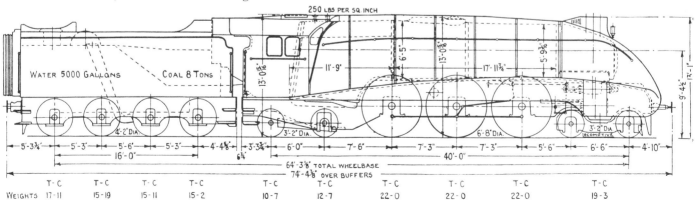

4-6-2 STREAMLINED LOCOMOTIVE, L.N.E.R.

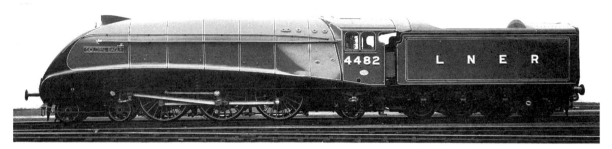

FOR the operation of the high-speed Silver Jubilee train service between King's Cross and Newcastle, begun on September 30, 1935, three streamlined Pacific locomotives were built at Doncaster to the designs of Sir Nigel Gresley, and others have been built since for the operation of the Coronation and the normal Anglo-Scottish expresses.

The boiler is of the tapered type with a maximum outside diameter of 6 ft. 5 in.; the back ring is tapered top and bottom and the front ring is parallel. The round topped wide firebox has a longer combustion chamber than the standard Pacifics, and has a grate area of 41.2 sq. ft. in conjunction with a heating surface of 231 sq. ft. The 121 tubes of 2¼ in. o.d. and the 43 flues of 5¼ in. o.d. contribute 2,345 sq. ft. to the evaporative total of 2,576 sq. ft. The length between tubeplates is 17 ft. 11¾ in. The double-beat regulator is located in a dome-cum-steam-collector on the tapered ring and feeds into an internal steam pipe of 7 in. diameter. After passage through the 43-element superheater the steam is led down three 5-in. pipes in the smokebox to the three cylinders. The superheating surface is 750 sq. ft. Alfol insulation is used for the boiler and firebox.

Three cylinders 18½ in. by 26 in. drive the centre pair of 6 ft. 8 in. coupled wheels. The steam and exhaust events are controlled by 9-in. piston valves actuated by two sets of Walschaerts gear with the Gresley arrangement of levers for transferring the motion to the inside valve. The valve gear throughout has ball and roller bearings at the joints. The valves have a steam lap of 1⅝ in., a maximum travel of 5¾ in., and a maximum cut-off of 65 per cent., and the reversing is of the vertical screw type. The exhaust steam is ejected through a blast pipe nozzle of 5¼ in. diameter which is provided with a Churchward jumper ring to relieve excessive back pressure. The top of the smokebox is cut away by the streamlining, and the casing has two hinged doors through which access can be gained to the smokebox door proper.

Vacuum braking is employed for both locomotive and train, the locomotive having three 21-in. cylinders providing a braking effort of 86 per cent. of the weight on the coupled wheels. The bogie and trailing wheels are not braked. The complete engine plus tender weight of the three *Silver Link* locomotives is 165.35 tons, and of th *Dominion of Canada* batch 167.1 tons. Since war began the valences above the rods have been removed.

Cab fittings include a regulator handle at each side connected by a cross-shaft; screw reverse, with indicating plate on the boiler back; pyrometer; Flaman speed indicator; live steam and exhaust steam injector handles; steam sanding handle; and bucket seats. The tender is of the non-bogie eight-wheeled corridor type with Pullman vestibule connection and Buckeye coupler. A flexible rubber roofing covers the gap between the front of the tender and the cab roof.

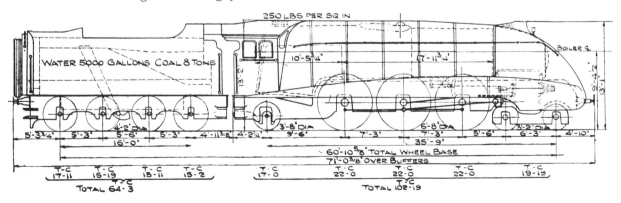

4-6-2 SUPER-PACIFIC LOCOMOTIVE, L.N.E.R.

KNOWN generally at the Super-Pacifics, the A3 class are a higher-pressure version of the 180 lb., or Class A1, Pacifics. They followed tests made with one of the latter class, No. 4480, *Enterprise*, which had its cylinders lined up and the boiler pressure increased. First built new in 1928, these engines closely resemble the A1 class in external appearance, but may be distinguished by a shallow curved casing on each side of the smokebox behind the chimney, which cover the ends of the large superheater header. Despite the construction of the streamlined Pacifics from 1935 onwards, it was the A3 class, working at 220 lb. pressure, that did the bulk of the hard work on the L.N.E.R. main line trains from London to Scotland and Yorkshire up to September, 1939.

The boiler is of the tapered type used on the A1 Pacifics, but with thicker plates. The external dimensions are the same, viz., 6 ft. 5 in. maximum diameter and 19 ft. between tubeplates. The barrel is formed of two plates, and contains 121 tubes of $2\frac{1}{4}$ in. o.d. and 43 flues of $5\frac{1}{4}$ in. o.d. located in five rows, which give heating surfaces of 1,399 and 1,123 sq. ft. respectively. With the addition of 215 sq. ft. from the round-topped wide firebox, the total evaporative surface is 2,737 sq. ft., the grate area is 41.25 sq. ft., and the superheating surface is 635 sq. ft. As with the A1 Pacifics, a short combustion chamber is incorporated in the firebox. Recently a tube and flue surface of 2,477 sq. ft. has been given officially, though the number and diameter remain unchanged.

The three 19 in. by 26 in. cylinders all drive the centre coupled axle; they have 8 in. piston valves driven by Walschaerts motion for the outside cylinders, and with Gresley levers for the inside valve, which give the usual maximum cut-off of 65 per cent. An axle load of just over 22 tons has been permitted in these engines, partly on account of the low hammer blow, which followed the Bridge Stress Committee's investigations. The hammer blow is 4.3 tons per wheel, 2.6 tons per axle, and 2.3 tons for the engine at 360 r.p.m. The adhesion weight is 66.2 tons and the total engine weight 96.25 tons. With 75 per cent. of the boiler pressure the tractive effort is 29,000 lb., resulting in a factor of adhesion of 5.1. The ordinary eight-wheeled tender fitted to these Super-Pacifics carries 5,000 gallons of water and 9 tons of coal ; it weighs 56.3 tons. The corridor tenders attached to some of the class have the same capacity, but weigh 62.4 tons, but other non-corridor tenders holding 8 tons of coal weigh 57.9 tons.

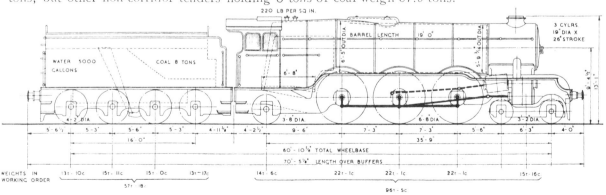

4-6-2 REBUILT LOCOMOTIVE, L.N.E.R.

ONE of the most interesting rebuilds ever undertaken in British locomotive practice was that initiated in 1943 on the L.N.E.R. under the ægis of Mr. E. Thompson, the Chief Mechanical Engineer, and comprising the conversion of Sir Nigel Gresley's three-cylinder P2 class 2-8-2 passenger engines to three-cylinder Pacifics. The first of the class to be so treated was No. 2005, built in 1936, and the conversion of the remaining five engines has been carried out subsequently. The rebuilt engines are being classified as A2, thus taking up the code number held by the erstwhile Pacifics of Sir Vincent Raven's design, all of which were scrapped during the Gresley regime. The official reason given for the conversion of the P2 Mikados to the 4-6-2 wheel arrangement was to extend their range of operation by reducing the coupled wheelbase to give more freedom round curves.

The rebuilt engines still have a taper boiler which is very much as in the original locomotives, but in order to straighten the steam pipes the barrel was shortened to give a length of 17 ft. between tubeplates. The working pressure was raised by 5 lb. to 225 lb. per sq. in. The heating surface of the flues is now 1,212 sq. ft., and that of the tubes 1,004 sq. ft.; the firebox heating surface remains as before at 237 sq. ft., so that the evaporative total is 2,453 sq. ft. Due to the shortening of the barrel, the superheating surface was reduced by about 100 sq. ft. to 680 sq. ft.

Although many of the original parts, including the outside coupling and connecting rods and the outside valve motion details, were used again, the Gresley conjugated motion for the inside valve was superseded by a separate set of Walschaerts motion driven by an eccentric. The new inside motion plate thereby made necessary is of welded construction, and it also forms the main front end support for the boiler.

The new bogie replacing the pony truck and leading coupled wheels of the original engine has horns, stays and central control box of welded construction. It is of the side support pattern in which the superimposed weight is taken through spherical surfaces on to bronze slippers located directly above the lines of the bogie frame plates. Side control is by means of helical springs given an initial compression of two tons; the maximum movement of the bogie is 4 in. on each side of the centre line. The original engine incorporated a spliced front end to the main locomotive frame, and it was simply a replacement of this portion that was needed in the main frame structure on rebuilding. Tractive effort at 75 per cent. of the boiler pressure is 35,500 lb., giving an adhesive factor of 4.18.

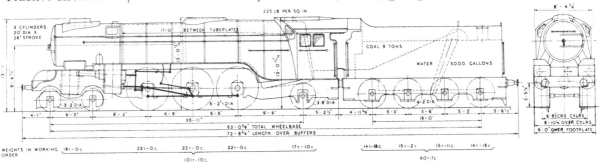

4-6-2 EXPRESS LOCOMOTIVE, L.N.E.R.

WITH the single exception of *The Great Bear* on the G.W.R., the Gresley Pacifics built at Doncaster in 1922 were the first engines of the 4-6-2 wheel arrangement to run in Britain, and they represented an increase of 50 per cent. over the previous G.N.R. main express class, the Ivatt Atlantics. They were designed to take 600-ton loads over the G.N.R. line from London to York, and although the type has been developed into the so-called Super-Pacifics with a higher boiler pressure, the 51 engines with a pressure of 180 lb. per sq. in. still operate in the heaviest duties and no distinction is drawn in making up the rosters. Slight detail changes were made in ensuing batches of the 180 lb. Pacifics—the whole series now being classified as A1—resulting in a trifling increase in weight. 220 lb. boilers are now being fitted to the A1 class engines, and of course give increased weight. Apparently the whole class is to be converted to A3.

The boiler has a maximum outside diameter of 6 ft. 5 in. at the firebox and the back ring tapers on top and bottom to fit over the parallel front ring, which has an outside diameter of 5 ft. 9 in. There are 168 tubes of $2\frac{1}{4}$ in. o.d. and 32 flues of $5\frac{1}{4}$ in. o.d. which are 19 ft. long, and which together give a heating surface of 2,715 sq. ft. The round-topped wide firebox incorporates a short combustion chamber and furnishes a heating surface of 215 sq. ft., making an evaporative total of 2,930 sq. ft. The grate area is 41.2 sq. ft. and the superheater surface is 525 sq. ft.

The three 20 in. by 26 in. cylinders all drive the centre coupled axle, the inside cylinder being inclined at 1 in 8. Each cylinder has an 8-in. piston valve the two outside valves being driven by Walschaerts gear and the inner valve by Gresley levers. The original valve travel and lap were lengthened after the comparative trials with a G.W.R. Castle 4-6-0. The full-gear cut-off is 65 per cent., and with the proportion of 75 per cent. of the boiler pressure—the maximum percentage which can be used with a 65 per cent. cut-off—the tractive effort is 26,400 lb. Against the adhesion weight of 60 tons of the earliest batch this gives a factor of adhesion of 5.15, or 5.2 against the 60.7 tons of some of the later engines. No. 4772 of this class just touched 100 m.p.h.

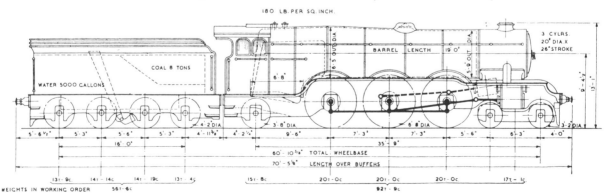

4-6-2 MIXED TRAFFIC LOCOMOTIVE, L.N.E.R.

IN 1944 the last four engines of a batch of 25 Green Arrow 2-6-2 locomotives being built at Darlington Works were materially altered in design, and appeared with the 4-6-2 wheel arrangement and major modifications in the driving gear. As with other locomotives to Mr. E. Thompson's design, the Gresley practice and tradition have gone by the board. The Gresley conjugated valve motion of the Green Arrow and other classes has been replaced by three separate sets of Walschaerts motion; the maximum cut-off is now 75 per cent. in place of 65 per cent.; screw reversing gear has given way to steam reversing apparatus; a double-exhaust system (the one successful feature Gresley did not incorporate in his V2 design) is fitted, in a very long smokebox; the drive from the three cylinders is now divided over two axles; the swing-link pony truck and swing-link bogie favoured by Gresley have given way to a bogie with spring side-control; the cylinder diameter has been increased by ½ in., and the boiler pressure by 5 lb. per sq. in., compared with the Green Arrow class; and the locomotive brakes are now steam operated, contrasted with Gresley's standard of the vacuum system. So much for the differences from the V2 class; the main similarity between the V2 class and these new A2/1 class Pacifics is the boiler, which from the front tubeplate backwards is the same in both types, except that the A2/1 engines have a rocking grate and a hopper ashpan. In general appearance the new Pacifics are not unlike the *Cock o' the North* rebuilds (see p. 23) but of course have a smaller firebox and grate than the A2 engines.

Boiler and heating surface particulars are the same as those given on p. 27 for the Green Arrow 2-6-2, except the working pressure is 225 lb. per sq. in. The two outside 19 in. by 26 in. cylinders drive the centre pair of 6 ft. 2 in. coupled wheels and the inside cylinder the leading coupled axle; but inside and outside connecting rods are the same length, and are much shorter than the outside rods of the V2. The outside cylinders are set close up against the leading coupled wheels, as in the Green Arrow class. The piston valves are 10 in. diameter and have a steam lap of 1⅝ in. and a maximum travel of 6¾ in. The maximum axle load of 22 tons is the same as that of the 2-6-2 engines, but the total engine weight of 98 tons is only five tons greater. At 75 per cent. of the boiler pressure the tractive effort is 32,000 lb., giving a factor of adhesion of 4.6.

The leading bogie retains the Gresley wheelbase of 6 ft. 3 in. and wheel diameter of 3 ft. 2 in., but is standard with the bogie of the B2 class *Antelope* 4-6-0 engines, and the weight is not taken through the centre pivot, but through hemispherical side bearers. The bogie frame stays, the engine spring and motion brackets and other parts are fabricated by welding. A standard 4,200-gal. six-wheel tender is attached.

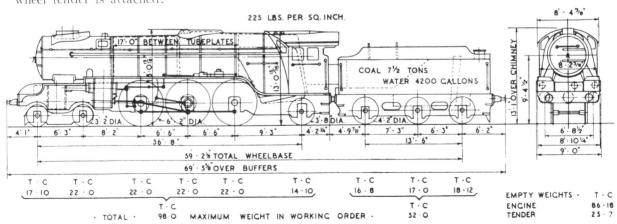

2-8-2 PASSENGER LOCOMOTIVE, L.N.E.R.

THERE have been six 2-8-2 passenger locomotives on the L.N.E.R., the first being No. 2001, *Cock o'
the North*, set to work in 1934. The second, No. 2002, *Earl Marischal*, was similar to *Cock o' the
North*, but had Walschaerts gear and piston valves in place of rotary cam poppet valves. The last
four, headed by No. 2003, *Lord President*, had piston valves and were also modified in various
particulars, the front ends, for example, being similar to those of the streamlined Pacifics. These
Mikado engines were designed for the operation of 500-ton express trains over the heavy grades,
with numerous slacks, between Edinburgh and Aberdeen. Under the responsibility of Mr. E.
Thompson, who became C.M.E. on the death of Sir Nigel Gresley, these engines have been
converted to the 4-6-2 wheel arrangement, and a description of the rebuild is given on page 23.
Rebuilding was undertaken at the Doncaster Plant.

Additional to the dimensions given on the diagram, *Lord President* had the following
characteristics: Three cylinders 21 in. by 26 in.; tube heating surface 2,477 sq. ft.; firebox heating
surface 237 sq. ft.; total evaporative heating surface 2,714 sq. ft.; grate area 50 sq. ft.; superheating surface 635 sq. ft.; double Kylchap blast pipe; 121 tubes $2\frac{1}{4}$ in. o.d.; 43 flues $5\frac{1}{4}$ in. o.d. The
sixth engine was fitted with a longer combustion chamber, which gave a total firebox heating surface
of 253 sq. ft. and a volume of 319 sq. ft. with the same grate area. *Cock o' the North* has recorded
a d.b.h.p. of 2,100 at a speed of 60 m.p.h. The tractive effort at 75 per cent. of the boiler pressure
was 38,400 lb. The usual Walschaerts-Gresley motion actuated the 9 in. piston valves, and other
standard L.N.E. details were piston and rod in one forging, 56 per cent. air space through the grate,
and three cylinders cast in one piece. *Cock o' the North* was heavier than the other engines, and
was the locomotive sent over to France for test on Vitry plant, and afterwards ran on the Paris-
Orleans section of the P.O. Midi Railway, a fairly straight line where the 19 ft. 6 in. coupled wheelbase did not cause the inconvenience it did subsequently on the sinuous Edinburgh-Aberdeen route.
The profile adopted for *Cock o' the North* was adapted later to the design of the streamlined
Pacifics. The tenders used were the same as those attached to the A3 class Super-Pacifics.

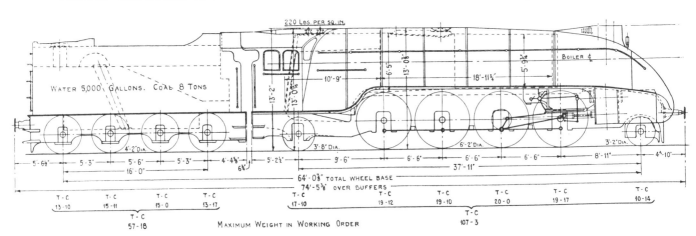

2-6-2 MAIN-LINE LOCOMOTIVE, L.N.E.R.

NAMED *Green Arrow*, the first of the now very numerous V2 class of 2-6-2, or "Prairie," engines on the L.N.E.R. system was built at Doncaster in 1936 to the requirements of the late Sir Nigel (then Mr. H. N.) Gresley, and incorporates most of that great locomotive engineer's standard features. It was intended for main-line trains of a weight and speed rather less than those within the Pacific range, at least as regards the A3 and A4 classes, but in the war years much of the main-line passenger traffic on the King's Cross to Yorkshire and Scotland routes has been handled by these locomotives, with train loads up to 700 tons or more made up of more than 20 passenger vehicles. As in the pre-war years, they still handle many heavy braked and unbraked freight trains. In 1944 the V2 design was modified into a 4-6-2 layout with 19-in. cylinders, three separate sets of valve gear, and divided drive; these engines are known as class A2/1.

The boiler design is based on that of the A3 class of Super-Pacifics, but the barrel is shorter. The outside diameter tapers from 5 ft. 9 in. in the front parallel ring to 6 ft. 5 in. at the throat plate; the barrel length is 17 ft. and the tube length the same. The round-topped, wide firebox has a heating surface of 215 sq. ft., the 2¼ in. tubes (121 in number) give 1,211 sq. ft., and the 5¼ in. flues (43 in number) 1,005 sq. ft., producing a total evaporative surface of 2,431 sq. ft. The grate area is 41.2 sq. ft. and the superheating surface 680 sq. ft. Two 3½ in. Ross pop safety valves are fitted, and the grate has narrow air-space bars giving air openings amounting to 56 per cent. of the total grate area.

A monobloc casting is used for the three 18½ in. by 26 in. cylinders, steam chests and smokebox saddle. The 9 in. piston valves are operated by Walschaerts gear with Gresley conjugating levers for the inside valve. The motion is arranged to give a maximum cut-off restricted to 65 per cent., the equivalent valve travel being 5⅝ in. All cylinders drive the centre coupled axle, the middle cylinder being raised well up and sloped sharply down so that its drive clears the leading coupled axle. All coupled axle journals are 9½ in. diameter by 11 in. long. Wheel, wheelbase and tender particulars are given on the accompanying diagram. The usual Gresley design of front pony truck and Cartazzi trailing axleboxes are embodied. Vacuum brake equipment is fitted to engine and tender, the engine having two 24 in. and the tender two 21 in. cylinders. At 75 per cent. of the working pressure of 220 lb. per sq. in. the tractive effort is 29,800 lb., and the corresponding factor of adhesion 4.95.

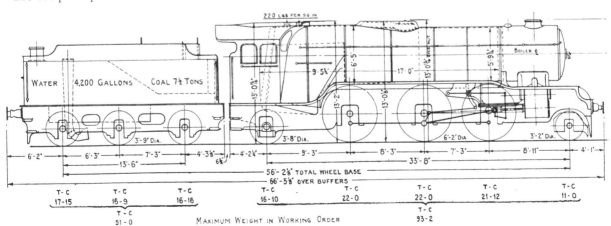

2-6-2 MEDIUM-WEIGHT LOCOMOTIVE, L.N.E.R.

LAST of all the many steam locomotive classes designed under the ægis of the late Sir Nigel Gresley was the *Bantam Cock* 2-6-2 type, classified V4 in the L.N.E.R. list. Intended to operate over the great majority of the company's lines, particularly where the heavier V2 engines could not run because of their 22-ton axle load, only two of the smaller engines were built before Sir Nigel's death, and no more have since been constructed. Most of the Gresley features, such as wide firebox, high boiler pressure, three cylinders, conjugated valve motion, long valve travel, steam collector, double-window cab, leading pony truck with three-pin hangers, and Cartazzi trailing boxes are incorporated. As a rule, these engines work in the Scottish area.

In order to keep down the weight, the boiler barrel is made of 2 per cent. nickel steel; it has a parallel front course, and the second course tapers top and bottom from 4 ft. 8 in. to 5 ft. 4 in. in outside diameter. A steam collector is fitted behind the dome, the steam going to a slide-valve regulator through a series of transverse slots $\frac{1}{2}$ in. wide. The first of the two V4 locomotives has a copper firebox and copper side stays, but the second locomotive has a welded steel box equipped with a Nicholson thermic syphon. In each case the grate area is 28.5 sq. ft. The boiler barrel contains 143 tubes of $1\frac{3}{4}$ in. o.d. and 22 flues of $5\frac{1}{4}$ in. o.d.; these give a heating surface of 1,292 sq. ft., and the firebox of the first engine gives an additional 152 sq. ft., making a total evaporative surface of 1,444 sq. ft. The surface of the AX-type superheater, with $1\frac{1}{8}$ in. elements, is 356 sq. ft. This superheater has isolated saturated and superheated compartments in the header.

The three 15 in. by 26 in. cylinders are cast monobloc with the smokebox saddle and valve chests, and are fitted with 7 in. piston valves operated by two outside sets of Walschaerts motion with Gresley levers for the inside valve. Each main piston head and rod is an integral steel forging connected to a three-bar crosshead. In addition to the revolving masses, 40 per cent. of the reciprocating weights are balanced by weights in the wheels; the reciprocating balance for the inside drive is confined to the driving wheels, but that of the outside lines is distributed over the coupled wheels. The journals of the coupled axles are $8\frac{3}{4}$ in. diameter by 9 in. long.

A standard swing-link pony truck with $4\frac{1}{2}$ in. play on either side carries the leading end of the engine, and at the back the trailing radial axle has Cartazzi boxes planed to an inclination of 1 in 10. These arrangements, and the short rigid wheelbase of 12 ft. 10 in., allow the engine to traverse curves of 4 chains radius. At 75 per cent. of the boiler pressure of 250 lb. the tractive effort is 24,200 lb., giving a factor of adhesion of 4.8.

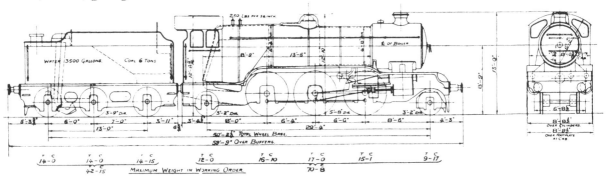

4-6-0 MIXED-TRAFFIC LOCOMOTIVE, L.N.E.R.

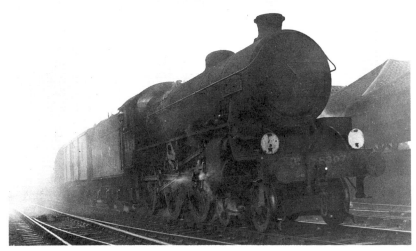

THE first really new locomotive design of Mr. E. Thompson after succeeding the late Sir Nigel Gresley as Chief Mechanical Engineer of the L.N.E.R. was a fast freight 4-6-0, the first of which, No. 8301 *Springbok*, was completed at the end of 1942. For the first time since the 1923 grouping a L.N.E.R. main-line class of locomotive was built with only two cylinders. The first batch of these engines was constructed at Darlington works, and they are intended to operate over nearly all of the company's lines. They have a nominal tractive effort under the usual rules which is inferior only to those of the Pacific and Green Arrow classes among the main-line passenger and mixed-traffic types on the L.N.E.R. A great effort was made to use existing patterns, jigs, tools and designs in order to save labour and material in war-time, but there has been one departure from normal locomotive constructional practice, and that is the extension of welding in place of the use of steel castings. Only the wheel centres, buffer sockets and horn blocks have been cast of steel. The cylinders are based on those of the old Great Northern two-cylinder Moguls, but with improved steam passages.

A boiler duplicate with that of the B.17 Sandringhams has been embodied, but the Ross pop safety valves have been set to lift at 225 lb. per sq. in. instead of at 200 lb. The barrel houses 143 tubes of 2 in. o.d. and 24 flues of $5\frac{1}{4}$ in. o.d., and the total evaporative surface is 1,676 sq. ft., made up as detailed in the description of the Sandringham passenger locomotives on page 31. Other boiler particulars will be found in the same place.

Steam is supplied to two 20 in. by 26 in. cylinders driving the centre pair of 6 ft. 2 in. wheels, and normal Walschaerts motion actuates the overhead piston valves. These valves are 10 in. in diameter, and have a steam lap of $1\frac{5}{8}$ in. and a maximum travel of $6\frac{5}{8}$ in. The full-gear cut-off is 75 per cent., and this is another difference compared with Gresley practice. All the coupled axles have journals $8\frac{3}{4}$ in. diameter by 9 in. long, and the main crankpins are $5\frac{1}{2}$ in. diameter by 6 in. long. The maximum axle load is only $17\frac{3}{4}$ tons, and against the adhesion weight of 52.5 tons the maximum tractive effort at 75 per cent. of the boiler pressure of 23,750 lb. gives an adhesive factor of 4.95 A steam brake is fitted to the engine, contrasted with the vacuum cylinders standard on previous engines.

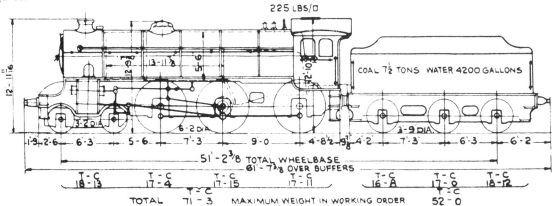

4-6-0 PASSENGER LOCOMOTIVE, L.N.E.R.

FOLLOWING certain bridge strengthening, a new type of 4-6-0 locomotive with three cylinders was built specially for the difficult East Anglian lines of the L.N.E.R. in 1928-29, and was dubbed the Sandringham class, after the name given to the first one, No. 2800. These engines are class B.17 in the L.N.E.R. list. The first ten were built by the North British Locomotive Co., Ltd., but others have been built since at the railway works. In 1937 two of the class were streamlined to work the East Anglian express.

The parallel boiler has a maximum diameter of 5 ft. 6 in. and contains 143 tubes of 2 in. o.d. and 24 flues of 5¼ in. o.d., which give heating surfaces of 1,048 and 460 sq. ft. respectively. Added to these, the firebox surface of 168 sq. ft. results in a total evaporative surface of 1,676 sq. ft. The grate area is 27.5 sq. ft., the working pressure 200 lb. per sq. in., and the superheating surface 344 sq. ft. The boiler barrel has a length of 13 ft. 6 in. and the tubes of 14 ft.

Similar in many mechanical details to the 4-4-0 Shire class, the B.17 engines have three 17½ in. by 26 in. cylinders; the outer pair drive the centre 6 ft. 8 in. coupled wheels, and the inside cylinder the leading coupled axle. The 8 in. inside-admission piston valves are driven by Walschaerts-Gresley motion, and the maximum cut-off is fixed at 65 per cent. The Gresley conjugating levers are located at the rear of the cylinders. Compared with the ex-G.E.R. two-cylinder 4-6-0 engines, the Sandringhams have a maximum axle load of 18.3 tons as against 16 tons and an engine weight of 76.75 tons to 77.25 tons against 63 tons; but owing to the high hammer blow of the older engines and the well-balanced design of the B.17 class, there is no increase in the maximum instantaneous wheel or axle loads. Empty, the locomotive alone scales 69.75 tons.

With the full-gear cut-off the tractive factor may be taken as 75 per cent. of the boiler pressure, and this gives a force at the wheel rims of 22,400 lb. and a factor of adhesion of 5.4. The six-wheel tender weighs 19 tons tare and 39.5 tons with the full complement of 3,700 gal. of water and 4 tons of coal; but Sandringhams working on sections of line other than the ex-G.E.R. are provided with tenders carrying 4,20 0 gal. of water and 7½ tons of coal; these tenders weigh 52.5 tons when full, and the combined e ngine and tender weight is then 129.75 tons.

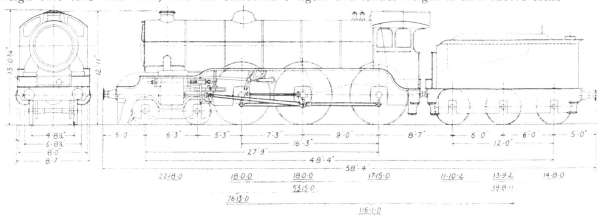

4-4-0 PASSENGER LOCOMOTIVE, L.N.E.R.

FOR the operation of lighter main-line expresses in the northern area and for general passenger work a batch of three-cylinder 4-4-0 engines—the first in Britain—was introduced by the L.N.E.R. in 1928, and named after counties served by L.N.E.R. lines. All the engines of the first batch had piston valves operated by Walschaerts gear outside and Gresley floating links for the inside valve. Succeeding batches had poppet valves of both oscillating cam and rotary cam types, but in the latest batch a return has been made to piston valves. The Shire class ranks second to the Southern Railway Schools class as the largest and most powerful 4-4-0 locomotive in Europe. Later engines have been named after well-known hunts along the L.N.E.R. system.

A parallel boiler with a round-topped firebox is fitted. The barrel has a maximum external diameter of 5 ft. 6 in. and contains 177 tubes of $1\frac{3}{4}$ in. o.d. and 24 flues of $5\frac{1}{4}$ in. o.d., which give a heating surface of 871 plus 355 = 1,226 sq. ft. To this must be added the 171 sq. ft. contributed by the firebox, giving a total evaporative surface of 1,397 sq. ft. The superheating surface is 246 sq. ft. and the grate area is 26 sq. ft. Some of the superheaters have a surface of 272 sq. ft. from 24 elements of $1\frac{1}{8}$ in. o.d. The normal length between the smokebox and firebox tubeplates is 10 ft. 9 in.

The three 17 in. by 26 in. cylinders are arranged in line above the bogie centre. Those with piston valves have a maximum cut-off of 65 per cent., in accordance with normal L.N.E.R. practice for express engines, but the poppet valve motions are arranged for a maximum cut-off of 75 per cent. In some of the engines the drive on to the outside crank pins is through the Woodard arrangement of rods, in which the big end is forked round the coupling rod and mounted on the same bush, thus transferring part of the piston load direct to the coupling rod without first passing it through the leading crankpin. At 75 per cent. of the boiler pressure of 180 lb. per sq. in. the tractive effort is 19,000 lb. The weight of the different batches varies from 64.6 to 66.0 tons and the adhesion weight from 41.2 to 42 tons. The tender is of very large capacity for a 4-4-0 engine and holds 4,200 gal. of water and $7\frac{1}{2}$ tons of coal; its weight is 52.7 tons fully laden, giving a maximum engine and tender weight of 118.7 tons. Some tenders scale 52 tons and the engine plus tender weight is 117.5 tons. One of these engines has been rebuilt as a two-cylinder machine.

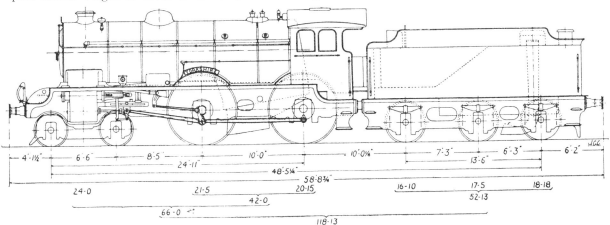

2-6-0 MAIN-LINE LOCOMOTIVE, L.N.E.R.

THE large number of three-cylinder 2-6-0 mixed traffic engines on the L.N.E.R. have their root in the celebrated Great Northern Railway Mogul No. 1000—the first locomotive in Britain with a 6 ft. boiler. It was put on the rails in 1920, and the basic dimensions of all the succeeding engines have been the same. The Great Northern engines were built at Doncaster, but since the 1923 amalgamation construction has been undertaken at the Darlington works also, and by locomotive manufacturers. The engines built since the amalgamation have been fitted with double-window cabs, and most of them have been cut down slightly in height to go within the composite loading gauge. They operate over all the main lines of the G.N., G.C., N.E., and N.B. sections, and seem to be used on nearly all types of freight and mineral traffic.

Only a single ring is used for the boiler barrel; it is $\frac{5}{8}$ in. thick, 6 ft. in outside diameter, and 11 ft. 6 in. long. The barrel houses 217 tubes of $1\frac{3}{4}$ in. o.d., which give a heating surface of 1,192 sq. ft., and 32 flues of $5\frac{1}{4}$ in. o.d., which provide a heating surface of 527 sq. ft. To this is added the 182 sq. ft. from the round-topped firebox, to give an evaporative total of 1,901 sq. ft. The 32 superheater elements of $1\frac{1}{8}$ in. inside diameter have a surface of 407 sq. ft., and the grate area is 28 sq. ft. The length between tubeplates is 12 ft.

All three cylinders have a common diameter and stroke of $18\frac{1}{2}$ and 26 in., and drive the centre coupled axle, the inside cylinder being set at an inclination of 1 in $8\frac{1}{2}$ to clear the leading coupled axle. G.N.R. No. 1000 was the first locomotive to have the Gresley gear for the inside cylinder with the cross levers in front of the cylinders. The maximum cut-off is 65 per cent., and with 75 per cent. of the boiler pressure the tractive effort is 26,500 lb., giving a factor of adhesion of 5 against the adhesion weight of 60.8 tons. The total engine weight is 72.6 tons. The earlier engines were supplied with 43-ton tenders carrying 3,500 gal. of water and $6\frac{1}{2}$ tons of coal, but the tenders of the later batches are duplicates of those of the Shire class; they weigh 52.7 tons and carry 4,200 gal. of water and 7.5 tons of coal, but some recent models scale only 51 tons when fully laden.

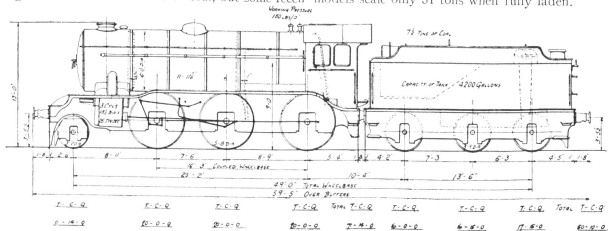

2-6-0 WEST HIGHLAND LOCOMOTIVE, L.N.E.R.

PARTICULARLY in the summer, traffic on the long West Highland line of the L.N.E.R., stretching from Glasgow to Fort William and Mallaig, had for some years grown beyond the capacity of a single locomotive if the principal trains were to be operated at anything but slow overall speeds. The long, steep grades called for adequate tractive and steaming power, but civil engineering considerations restricted the concentration of weight. After the amalgamation, the old North British 4-4-0 engines gradually gave place to ex-G.N.R. two-cylinder Moguls of the K2 class for the heaviest loads, but double-heading still was not unusual. The heavier K3 Moguls, with 6 ft. boilers and 60 tons of adhesion weight, cannot be used because of the high individual axle load and the heavy weight per foot run of wheelbase. Therefore, in 1937, the late Sir Nigel Gresley introduced a new 2-6-0 engine, *Loch Long*, classified K4 in the L.N.E.R. list, in order to provide the maximum drawbar pull at all speeds up to about 60 m.p.h. within the imposed engineering restrictions, which appear to have been modified, as a maximum axle load of 19.85 tons is permitted. Overall, the specific weight per unit of length is about 10 per cent. less than that of the K3 class, but this is due mainly to the smaller tender.

The grate area of 27.5 sq. ft. is practically the same as that of the K3 engines, and the working pressure of 180 lb. per sq. in. is the same. The 5 ft. 6 in. barrel is 11 ft. 1 in. long and contains 24 flues $5\frac{1}{4}$ in. o.d. and 164 tubes $1\frac{5}{8}$ in. o.d., 11 ft. 7 in. long; these give an evaporative surface of 1,254 sq. ft. and the firebox provides 168 sq. ft. towards the total heating surface of 1,422 sq. ft. The 24 elements of $1\frac{1}{8}$ in. o.d. give a superheating surface of 310 sq. ft. The firebox is of the round-top type with sloping grate, sloping back plate and sloping throat plate, and on the top wrapper are two Ross pop safety valves.

Though the engine wheelbase is the same as that of the K3 locomotives, the coupled wheels are only 5 ft. 2 in. diameter as against the 5 ft. 8 in. of the bigger engines, and it is this feature which provides the nominally greater starting tractive effort of 29,000 lb. at 75 per cent. boiler pressure, for the three $18\frac{1}{2}$ in. by 26 in. cylinders and the 180 lb. pressure are the same as in the big mixed-traffic engines. The drive of the three cylinders is concentrated on the centre coupled axle, and the piston valves are actuated by two outside sets of Walschaerts motion with Gresley conjugating levers for the inside valve. The construction of the leading pony truck, double-window cab, etc., are along Gresley standard lines, but the overall height from rail level is only 12 ft. $10\frac{1}{2}$ in.

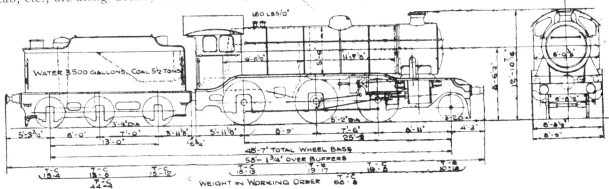

0-6-0 FREIGHT LOCOMOTIVE, L.N.E.R.

BEGINNING in 1926, a large number of big-boilered 0-6-0 locomotives have been built by the L.N.E.R., principally at Darlington works. They are of two classes, J38 and J39, the former having 4 ft. 8 in. wheels and the latter 5 ft. 2 in. wheels. They are virtually the same otherwise, but the illustrations depict the J39 series, which are intended for use on faster trains than the class with 4 ft. 8 in. wheels. Both types may be regarded as modern developments of the large-boilered P2 and P3 mineral engines of the old North Eastern Railway, rather than of the large six-coupled types of the old Great Eastern Railway, which, for example, have a much longer wheelbase, viz., 18 ft. 10 in. Class J38 was intended for the North British section.

The boiler barrel is in a single ring of 5 ft. 6 in. diameter outside. It contains 177 steel tubes of $1\frac{3}{4}$ in. o.d. and 24 flues of $5\frac{1}{4}$ in. o.d. which provide heating surfaces of 872 and 354 sq. ft. respectively, the length between tubeplates being 10 ft. 9 in. The evaporative total of 1,397 sq. ft. is made up by the addition of 171 sq. ft. from the firebox, which is of unusually large proportions for an ordinary main line goods engine, and carries on the tradition of ample steam raising capacity originated by the North Eastern engines mentioned above. The M.L.S. superheater comprises 24 elements with an outside diameter of $1\frac{1}{2}$ in. which give a superheating surface of 272 sq. ft. The header carries a snifting valve, which is located just behind the chimney. The round-top firebox has a sloping back plate, and also a sloping grate with an area of 26 sq. ft.

The two 20 in. by 26 in. cylinders are cast in one piece with their piston valve chambers and smokebox saddle. The valves are actuated by Stephenson link motion fitted with power reversing gear. The locomotive is braked on the Westinghouse air system and the tender with hand screw apparatus ; vacuum equipment is included in order to operate the train brakes when working braked stock or passenger trains. At 75 per cent. of the working pressure the tractive effort is 22,650 lb., giving an adhesion factor of 5.7. The tender is one of the L.N.E.R.'s standard patterns with water pick-up gear. The J38 class, with 4 ft. 8 in. wheels, weighs 58.95 tons and has a maximum axle load of 20.3 tons; the tenders, too, are bigger, weighing 52.5 tons and holding 4,200 gal. of water and $7\frac{1}{2}$ tons of coal, but some of the J39 class now have this type of tender.

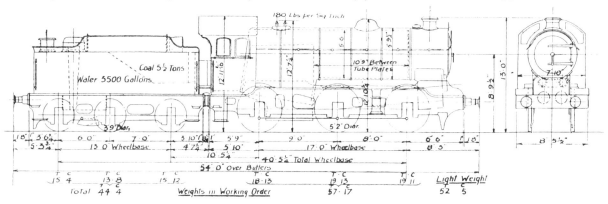

2-8-0 MINERAL LOCOMOTIVE, L.N.E.R.

THE numerous 3-cylinder Consolidation mineral engines of the L.N.E.R. can be traced back to the ex-G.N.R. 2-8-0 locomotive No. 461, built in 1918, which was the first locomotive to be fitted with Gresley conjugated valve motion. Actually, the arrangement adopted consisted of a number of links *behind* the piston valves, and the present arrangement of horizontal levers *in front* of the valves, standard on many classes of passenger and goods locomotives, was adopted first for the G.N.R. 3-cylinder Moguls of the 1000 class and the next batch of 2-8-0 coal engines, both of which were built in 1921. One rather unusual feature is the very small diameter of the leading pony truck wheels, viz., 2 ft. 8 in. Engines of this class have been built at Doncaster works during the war years, but the latest L.N.E.R. eight-coupled freight locomotives are the class O4 Thompson rebuilds from the G.C. Consolidations.

In general layout and dimensions the latest Consolidations differ only in detail from the 1921 series. The parallel boiler barrel has a maximum outside diameter of 5 ft. 6 in. and a length of 15 ft. $5\frac{1}{2}$ in., and it is riveted to a round-top firebox having a grate area of 27.5 sq. ft. and a heating surface of 163 sq. ft. The barrel contains 162 tubes of 2 in. o.d. and 24 flues of $5\frac{1}{4}$ in. o.d. which give respectively 1,338 and 524 sq. ft. of heating surface; the total evaporative surface is 2,024 sq. ft., and the superheating surface is 570 sq. ft. The barrel is covered with magnesia sectional lagging and the firebox with asbestos mattresses. The latest boilers have 160 tubes, 24 flues, an evaporative surface of 2,032 sq. ft., a superheater surface of 430 sq. ft., and a length between tubeplates of 16 ft. Feedwater heaters of the Dabeg and Worthington types have been tried on this class of locomotive.

The three cylinders are $18\frac{1}{2}$ in. by 26 in., and are provided with 8 in. piston valves actuated by two sets of Walschaerts gear with Gresley levers for the inside valve. The maximum valve travel is $5\frac{1}{4}$ in. and the steam lap $1\frac{1}{4}$ in.; negative lap to the extent of $\frac{1}{4}$ in. is provided. All three cylinders drive the second coupled axle, but the outside pair are almost horizontal, whereas the inside cylinder is inclined at 1 in 8. At the rim of the 4 ft. 8 in. wheels a tractive effort of 32,200 lb. is exerted assuming 75 per cent. of the boiler pressure of 180 lb. per sq. in., and this gives an adhesion factor of 5.3 to the weight of 67.15 tons on the coupled wheels. The total engine weight is 75.4 tons and that of the tender 43.1 tons when loaded with 6.5 tons of coal and 3,500 gal. of water. The latest engines, with double window cabs, weigh 78.6 tons, of which 69.3 tons are available for adhesion; and they haul 4,200 gal. tenders weighing $51\frac{1}{2}$ tons when carrying the full tanks and $7\frac{1}{2}$ tons of coal.

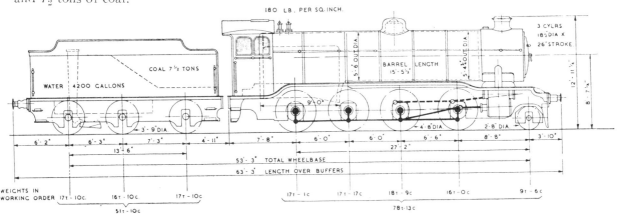

2-6-2T PASSENGER LOCOMOTIVE, L.N.E.R.

A BIG advance in the size and power of suburban passenger tank engines on the L.N.E.R. was made in 1930 with the construction at Doncaster of the first of the V1 class 2-6-2T locomotives. These engines have been built in several batches, and are allocated mainly to the southern Scottish and Tyneside areas. Originally their weight, maximum axle load (19.25 tons) and length did not permit them to operate on London suburban services such as those out of Liverpool Street. The design exhibits many of the Gresley standard features, such as three simple cylinders with two sets of Walschaerts gear; connecting rod big ends with non-adjustable floating bushes; single-throw crank axle of the balanced type; and a leading pony truck with swing links of the three-pin pattern. From 1935 onwards some of these engines have worked in the Great Eastern area also; and in the North Eastern area they are used on inter-urban services.

The parallel boiler barrel has an external diameter of 5 ft. and a length between tubeplates of 12 ft. 2 in. The tubes and flues, both of steel, give a heating surface of 1,198 sq. ft. and the copper inside firebox has a surface of 127 sq. ft., producing an evaporative total of 1,325 sq. ft. The 22-element superheater has a header of the Robinson pattern and a superheating surface of 284 sq. ft. A partial drop grate, with an area of 22 sq. ft., is fitted; it is screw-operated from the cab and counterbalanced by a helical spring. The boiler barrel has 149 tubes of $1\frac{3}{4}$ in. o.d. and 22 flues of $5\frac{1}{4}$ in. o.d.; the superheater elements are $1\frac{1}{8}$ in. o.d.

The three 16 in. by 26 in. cylinders together with their valve chests, steam and exhaust passages, are formed of a monobloc iron casting. The two outside cylinders and all the valve chests are set at an inclination of 1 in 30; the inside cylinder is inclined at 1 in 8. Gresley levers transfer the motion of the outside Walschaerts gear to the inside valve. A maximum valve travel of $6\frac{5}{16}$ in. in conjunction with a maximum cut-off of 68 per cent. is provided. At 75 per cent. of the 180 lb. boiler pressure, the tractive effort is 19,750 lb., giving a factor of adhesion of 6.5 against the adhesion weight of 57 tons with tanks full. With 2,000 gal. of water in the side and rear tanks the total engine weight is 84 tons; with the engine in the empty condition it is 66.7 tons. Steam brakes are fitted to the coupled wheels and vacuum apparatus for the train brakes is incorporated. Sixty per cent. of the reciprocating weights are balanced. In 1939 ten engines with 200 lb. per sq. in boiler pressure and weighing 86.6 tons were built, and classified as V3.

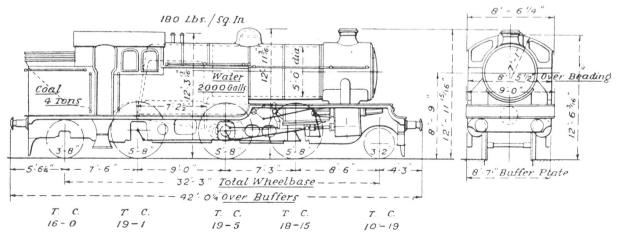

0-6-2T SUBURBAN LOCOMOTIVE, L.N.E.R.

FOR many years the suburban traffic over the steeply-graded branches leading from King's Cross to the northern heights of London has been worked by 0-6-2T engines, the first of which was introduced by Mr. Ivatt. A distinct advance was made in 1920 by fitting an enlarged superheated boiler at a high pitch and bigger cylinders, which of course led to an increase in the adhesion weight. Further engines built subsequently have followed the 1920 design with various minor modifications. Some of the engines are fitted with condensing pipes, through which the exhaust steam can be led into the water tanks when the engine is working through the Metropolitan tunnels.

The boiler is 4 ft. 8 in. in diameter and has a length of 10 ft. 1 in. The barrel houses 107 tubes of $1\frac{3}{4}$ in. o.d. and 34 flues of 4 in. o.d., which give heating surfaces of 510 and 370 sq. ft. respectively. To the total evaporative surface of 998 sq. ft. the round-top firebox contributes 118 sq. ft. The grate area is 19 sq. ft. and the working pressure 170 lb. per sq. in. A superheating surface of 207 sq. ft. is furnished by 17 twin-tube elements, each of which goes through two flues; these flues thus have only two $1\frac{1}{2}$ in. diameter elements in a cross section of about 11 sq. in.

The two 19 in. by 26 in. cylinders have 8 in. piston valves overhead; these valves are driven by Stephenson's link motion giving a maximum travel of $4\frac{7}{8}$ in. and a full gear cut-off of 75 per cent.; the steam lap is $1\frac{1}{8}$ in. and the negative exhaust lap $\frac{1}{8}$ in. Independent laminated springs are fitted below the leading and trailing pairs of 5 ft. 8 in. coupled wheels and helical springs beneath the driving boxes. The braking is on the vacuum system with the force provided by two 21 in. cylinders, and a hand brake is fitted also; the trailing radial wheels are unbraked. With the tanks holding the full complement of 2,000 gal. of water and the bunker 4 tons of coal the adhesion weight is 56.8 tons. Against this the tractive effort at 75 per cent. of the boiler pressure is 17,550 lb., giving a factor of adhesion of 7.25.

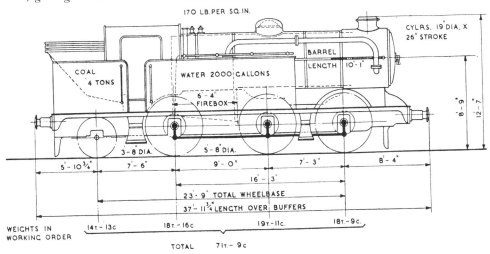

4-6-0 KING CLASS LOCOMOTIVE, G.W.R.

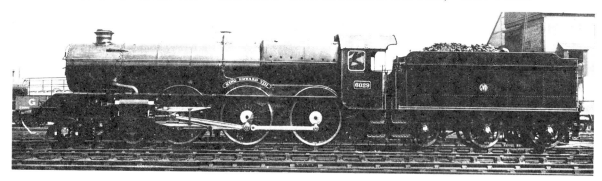

AS a reply to the L.N.E.R. Pacifics, the Southern Lord Nelsons, and the L.M.S.R. Royal Scots, and as a development of the Castles, which were limited to a maximum load of 315 tons between Taunton and Plymouth, the King class 4-6-0 locomotives were built at Swindon in 1927. They are the super Great Western engines in all respects, for they embody little that is new in their design, and are the culminating stage in the four-cylinder six-coupled G.W. engines, which began with the Stars in 1906, and passed through the Queen, Princess, Abbey, and Castle classes up to 1924. They are the latest type of express passenger engine to be designed and built for the Great Western system, and are the heaviest 4-6-0 locomotives in Britain.

The domeless boiler of the King class tapers from 5 ft. 6¼ in. at the smokebox to 6 ft. 0 in. outside diameter at the firebox throatplate. The barrel contains 171 tubes of 2¼ in. o.d. and 16 flues of 5⅛ in. o.d., which together give a heating surface of 2,007 sq. ft. The firebox has a heating surface of 194 sq. ft., giving a total evaporative surface of 2,201 sq. ft. The Swindon superheater has a surface of 313 sq. ft. The Belpaire narrow firebox has a length outside of no less than 11 ft. 6 in. and has a grate area of 34.3 sq. ft., the largest in Britain with a narrow box. Exhaust and live steam injectors are used to feed the water to the top feed valves and trays. The superheater comprises triple elements of 1 in. o.d. The distance between tubeplates is 16 ft. 5½ in.

The four 16¼ in. by 28 in. cylinders have the usual G.W.R. divided drive arrangement with piston valves driven by two sets of Walschaerts gear driven by eccentrics on the leading coupled axle. The inside connecting rods have adjustable big ends, but the outside rods are of the solid bushed pattern. The bogie wheelbase has been increased from the standard figure of 7 ft. to 7ft. 8 in.; outside bearings were preferred, but the rear bogie wheels have inside bearings as the outside pattern could not clear the outside cylinders. The axle load of 22.5 tons, giving an adhesion weight of 67.5 tons, was the heaviest in Britain in 1927, and even now is exceeded only by the L.M.S.R. Turbomotive. At 75 per cent. of the boiler pressure of 250 lb. per sq. in. the tractive effort is 35,600 lb., giving a factor of adhesion of 4.25. To the engine weight of 89 tons must be added the 46.7 tons of the standard self-trimming 4,000-gal. tender as fitted to the Castle class, giving a total engine plus tender weight of 135.7 tons.

The balancing of the King engines is typical of British express locomotives since the Bridge Stress Committee's investigation. The hammer blow per wheel does not exceed 1.79 tons, and per axle 2.8 tons; the total engine hammer blow is only 1.54 tons. These values are taken at 70 m.p.h. The proportion of reciprocating weights balanced is 34 per cent. inside and 42 per cent. outside. The inside balance is divided between leading and trailing coupled wheels only.

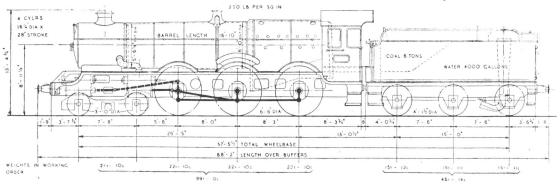

4-6-0 CASTLE CLASS LOCOMOTIVE, G.W.R.

ONE of the most efficient of all the Great Western express types is the Castle class, post-1918 development of the numerous four-cylinder 4-6-0 engines of the Star, Princess and Queen classes built between 1905 and 1914. In the matter of high speed they are the successors of the two-cylinder Saints and Courts, and they are the usual engines for such trains as the Cheltenham Flier. Several of the older four-cylinder 4-6-0 engines have been rebuilt as Castles, as has also the celebrated 4-6-2, *The Great Bear.*

The taper boiler is not standard with any other Great Western class, although the firebox is virtually the same as that of the 4700 class 2-8-0. Within a length of 14 ft. 10 in. the barrel tapers from an outside diameter of 5 ft. 9 in. at the back to 5 ft. 2 in. at the front, and is joined to a Belpaire firebox with a maximum outside length of 10 ft. The barrel has 197 tubes of 2 in. o.d. and 14 flues of $5\frac{1}{8}$ in. o.d., which are 15 ft. 3 in. long and give an aggregate heating surface of 1,857 sq. ft. The firebox contributes 163 sq. ft. to the total evaporative surface of 2,020 sq. ft., and has a grate area of 29.4 sq. ft. The usual moderate-degree Swindon superheater is fitted and each flue contains three elements making one return pass, or six element tubes per flue, the superheating surface being 262 sq. ft.

The four cylinders are arranged for divided drive, the inside pair driving the leading coupled axle and the outside pair the centre coupled axle. The 16 in. by 26 in. cylinders have piston valves driven by two sets of Walschaerts gear between the frames, the motion being transmitted to the front of the outside valves by horizontal rocking levers. The double-throw crank axle is of the built-up balanced type with the 6 ft. $8\frac{1}{2}$ in. wheels forced on. At 75 per cent. of the boiler pressure of 225 lb. per sq. in. the tractive effort is 27,900 lb., and as the adhesion weight is 58.8 tons the factor of adhesion is 4.73. The total engine weight is 79.85 tons. The original Castles were provided with 3,500-gal. tenders holding 6 tons of coal and weighing 40 tons. With these tenders the total weight was thus 119.85 tons. In 1927, the new Castles were supplied with a new self-trimming tender holding 4,000 gal. of water and weighing 46.7 tons, giving an engine plus tender weight of 126.55 tons. The illustrations on this page show the big tender combination, the total engine and tender wheelbase being only $\frac{1}{4}$ in. more than in the original series. A height reduced to 13 ft. 2 in. is a feature of the latest construction.

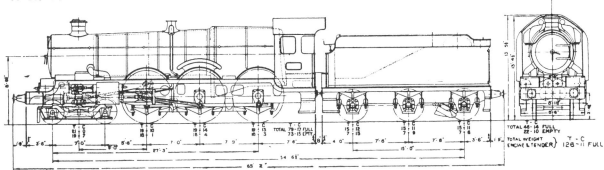

4-6-0 HALL CLASS LOCOMOTIVE, G.W.R.

WHEN early in 1928 the construction of a new and more powerful mixed traffic class was under consideration at Swindon, the two-cylinder 4-6-0 express engine *Saint Martin* was fitted with coupled wheels of 6 ft. diameter in place of the original 6 ft. 8½ in. set. Observations on its capacity led to the now numerous Hall class of 4-6-0, which are fitted with standard boilers used on the 2800 Consolidations, and the four-cylinder and two-cylinder 4-6-0's of the Star, Princess and Court classes. The Hall class are used largely on semi-fast and excursion trains, and are by no means unknown on express work. But their maximum axle load of 18.95 tons and weight of 3.83 tons per foot run of coupled wheelbase restricts the routes over which they can be used, compared with the Grange and Manor classes. One of the 1944 improved Halls is shown above.

The domeless taper boiler contains 176 tubes of 2 in. o.d. and 14 flues of 5⅛ in. o.d. which give an aggregate heating surface of 1,686 sq. ft. The total evaporative surface is brought up to 1,841 sq. ft. by the addition of 155 sq. ft. from the Belpaire firebox, which has a grate area of 27 sq. ft. The usual moderate-degree Swindon superheater is incorporated, with six 1.0-in. tube sections per flue giving a total of 262 sq. ft. of superheating surface. The length between tube-plates is 15 ft. 2⅛ in., and the boiler barrel, with a length of 14 ft. 10 in., tapers from 5 ft. 6 in. o.d. at the back to 4 ft. 10¾ in. at the front. The length of 14 ft. 10 in. is standard for many Great Western main-line classes, even when the boiler diameters and proportions are not the same, and dates from Churchward's early Consolidation and 4-6-0 classes.

Two outside cylinders 18½ in. by 30 in. drive the centre coupled wheels. They are fitted with overhead piston valves driven by independent sets of Stephenson link motion driven from the second coupled axle, the motion being transferred outside the frame by rocking shafts. At 75 per cent. of the boiler pressure of 225 lb. per sq. in. the tractive effort is 24,100 lb., giving an adhesion factor of 5.25 against the weight of 56.5 tons resting on the coupled wheels. The engine weight is 75 tons full and 69 tons empty. The earlier engines of the class were fitted with 3,500-gal. tenders weighing 40 tons, and giving an engine plus tender weight of 115 tons. The later machines have been provided with 4,000-gal. tenders scaling 46.7 tons, and giving an engine plus tender total of 121.7 tons. Certain constructiona modifications were made in new Halls in 1944, each main frame now being in one length throughout, the bogie having four independent laminated bearing springs, and the superheater being of the 21-flue type with four element passes per flue.

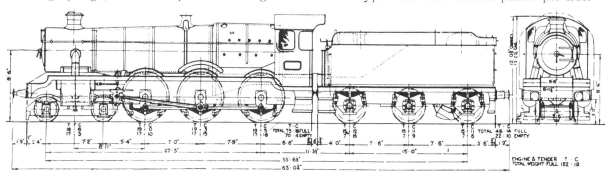

4-6-0 FAST GOODS LOCOMOTIVES, G.W.R.

AFTER 25 years of a general usefulness which probably has not been exceeded on British railways, some of the Great Western Moguls have been broken up and their place is being taken by a new type of express freight engine which is almost a duplicate of those of the well-known Hall class, but with 5 ft. 8 in. wheels instead of 6 ft. The boilers, wheelbase, bogies, motion, and cab are the same. The cylinders are of the same dimensions as in the Hall class, but are to an improved design, and the tender has a capacity of 3,500 gal. compared with 4,000 gal. Known as the Grange class, the new locomotives are intended for fast freight traffic, more particularly the broccoli traffic from Cornwall and the fruit trains from Worcestershire and the Cotswolds.

The No. 1 standard boiler tapers from 5 ft. 6 in. to 4 ft. 10¾ in. in outside diameter within a length of 14 ft. 10 in. The tube and flue heating surface aggregates 1,686 sq. ft. and the firebox heating surface 155 sq. ft., giving an evaporative surface of 1,841 sq. ft. The tube, flue and superheater particulars are referred to in the description of the Hall class. The grate area is 27 sq. ft. and the superheating surface 262 sq. ft., while the usual G.W.R. fittings such as the top feed are incorporated.

The two 18½ in. by 30 in. cylinders produce a tractive effort of 26,450 lb. at the rims of the 5 ft. 8 in. wheels assuming 75 per cent. of the working pressure of 225 lb. per sq. in. The factor of adhesion is 4.85 related to the adhesion weight of 55.2 tons. The overhead piston valves are actuated by Stephenson's link motion. Six tons of coal and 3,500 gal. of water are carried in the six-wheeled tender, and water pick-up apparatus is fitted. A diagram of the Grange class is presented on this page.

A similar, but smaller, class, the Manors, was introduced in 1930, and is illustrated by the photograph on this page. The boiler tapers from 5 ft. 3 in. to 4 ft. 7⅝ in. in o.d., has a heating surface of 1,425 sq. ft., of which 140 sq. ft. comes from the firebox, a grate area of 22 sq. ft., and a superheating surface of 190 sq. ft. There are 158 tubes of 2 in. o.d. and 12 flues of 5⅛ in. o.d., 13 ft. long. The two 18 in. by 30 in. cylinders drive 5 ft. 8 in. coupled wheels spread over a base of 14 ft. 9 in., the engine plus tender wheelbase is 52 ft. 1¼ in., and the overall length 61 ft. 9¼ in. In working order the locomotive weighs 68.9 tons, of which 50.4 tons are adhesive; fully laden, the 3,500 gal. tender weighs 40 tons. At 75 per cent. of the working pressure of 225 lb. the tractive effort is 24,100 lb.

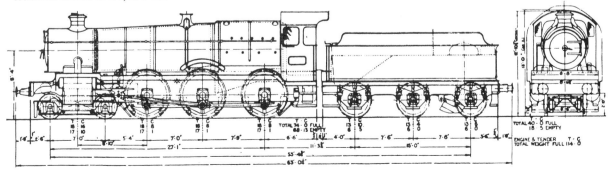

2-6-0 MIXED-TRAFFIC LOCOMOTIVE, G.W.R.

BEST-KNOWN and most numerous of all the Great Western fast goods and mixed traffic locomotives are the outside-cylinder Moguls which began with the 4300 class in the pre-1914 part of
Mr. Churchward's regime.   Eventually the class numbered 322 locomotives, but some have now
been scrapped and their places allocated to new 4-6-0 engines of the Grange class.   Some of the
Moguls were modified slightly as to weight distribution and were fitted with cabs having single
side windows; they are numbered in the 8300's.   The Moguls work all types of traffic, even to
express passenger trains like the Devonian, and during the course of the Bridge Stress Committee's
investigations one of them attained a speed of 85 m.p.h.

  There have been sundry slight differences in the weight and heating surfaces in the various
batches, which have been built not only at Swindon (43XX, 53XX, and 73XX types), but also at
the Darlington works of Robert Stephenson & Co. Ltd. (63XX), and the latter engines scale about
64 tons compared with the 62 tons of the standard Swindon built engines, and 65.3 tons of the
single-window cab type.   The taper boiler is the same as that used in the 3150 class of 2-6-2 tanks
and in the 2-8-0 tanks, and has outside diameters of 5 ft. 6 in. at the back and 4 ft. 10¾ in. at the
front.   The tube heating surface of 1,350 sq. ft. is obtained from 235 tubes of 1⅝ in. o.d. and 14
flues of 5⅛ in. o.d. with a length of 11 ft. 4½ in. The firebox heating surface is 129 sq. ft. and
the evaporative total 1,479 sq. ft. A grate area of 20.6 sq. ft. is provided.

  At 75 per cent. of the working pressure of 200 lb. per sq. in. the two 18½ in. by 30 in. cylinders produce a tractive effort of 22,600 lb. at the rims of the 5 ft. 8 in. wheels, and this gives a
factor of adhesion of 5.15 against the 52 tons resting on the coupled wheels, or 5.35 in the
engines with 54.3 tons of adhesion.

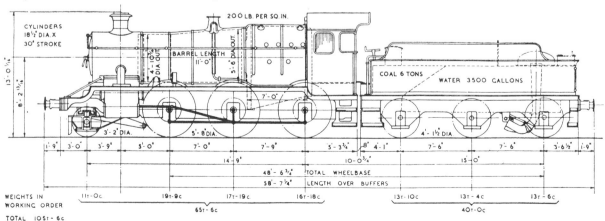

0-6-0 GOODS LOCOMOTIVE, G.W.R.

A SERIES of 20 light goods engines of the 0-6-0 wheel arrangement with taper boilers was built at Swindon Works in 1930. These engines may be considered as developments of the 41-ton 0-6-0 engines of the Midland & South Western Junction Railway which were rebuilt with taper boilers and other Great Western details at Swindon in 1926. The 1930 engines are numbered 2251-2270 and have replaced some of the old double-framed 0-6-0 goods locomotives. They are the only 0-6-0 taper boiler engines designed for the G.W.R. since the 1923 grouping. A further batch of these light-weight locomotives was constructed at Swindon works in 1944-45. The restricted height and width makes these engines suitable for many small lines.

The boiler is the standard No. 10 tapered pattern, but it is not used on any other purely Great Western class, although employed in the Swindon rebuilds of some of the ex-Taff Vale Railway and M. & S.W.J.R. engines. The barrel tapers from 5 ft. $0\frac{1}{2}$ in. o.d. at the back to 4 ft. $5\frac{1}{8}$ in. at the front in a length of 10 ft. 3 in. The tubes are 10 ft. $7\frac{1}{4}$ in. long and are 218 in number, of $1\frac{5}{8}$ in. o.d.; there are also six flues of $5\frac{1}{8}$ in. o.d. Tubes and flues have an aggregate heating surface of 1,069 sq. ft., and the firebox 102 sq. ft., giving a total evaporative surface of 1,171 sq. ft. The grate area is 17.4 sq. ft. and the working pressure 200 lb. per sq. in. The superheating surface is 76 sq. ft. obtained from the usual six 1.0-in. elements per flue of the Swindon superheater. Top-feed apparatus of the usual G.W.R. pattern is fitted to the safety-valve casing, the trays being located just beneath.

The $17\frac{1}{2}$ in. by 24 in. inside cylinders are similar to those of the 5700 class of 0-6-0 pannier tanks, but are cast integral with the smokebox saddle. The Stephenson link motion of both types is the same. The coupled wheels are 5 ft. 2 in. in diameter. At 75 per cent. of the boiler pressure the tractive effort is 17,775 lb., giving an adhesion factor of 5.45. A six-wheeled tender carrying 3,000 gal. of water and 5 tons of coal is attached; it is fitted with water pick-up apparatus and weighs 36.75 tons when full. The engine has a steam brake with equalised rigging, and vacuum apparatus is installed for the train brakes. The overall width of engine and tender is limited to 8 ft. 5 in. The tenders now used are of the flush-bottom pattern and have extended coal rails along the side of the bunker.

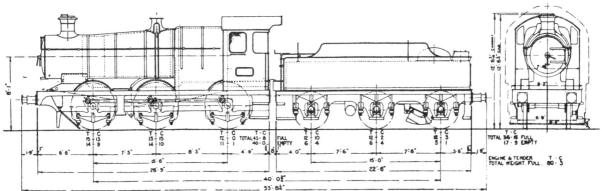

2-8-0 MINERAL LOCOMOTIVE, G.W.R.

THE earliest of the still existing Churchward standard locomotive types is the 2-8-0 coal engine class, the first of which originally was numbered 97. It was soon renumbered 2800, and altogether 84 of these machines have been built at Swindon, and numbered 2800-2883. They have been used for hauling 100-wagon coal trains from South Wales up to London, and although they are fitted with vacuum brake connections they are used almost exclusively on mineral trains. Since their inception the arrangement of the boiler heating surfaces has been changed, although the dimensions of the shell have remained the same. The early boilers were duplicates of those fitted to the erstwhile Atlantics and the first four-cylinder 4-6-0's. Engines with single-window cabs and numbered 2884 and upwards were built at Swindon in 1938.

The present boiler is the No. 1 standard as fitted to the Saint, Court, Star, Hall, and Grange classes. It tapers from 5 ft. 6 in. to 4 ft. $10\frac{3}{4}$ in. outside diameter, carries a working pressure of 225 lb. per sq. in., and has a tube plus flue heating surface of 1,686 sq. ft. The evaporative total of 1,841 sq. ft. is made up by the addition of 155 sq. ft. from the firebox. The grate area is 27 sq. ft. and the superheating surface 262 sq. ft. The boilers as first fitted about thirty years ago were of the non-superheated type, the total heating surface was 2,142 sq. ft., and the working pressure was 200 lb. per sq. in. Beginning in 1907 the working pressure was raised to 225 lb. In the present boilers there are 176 tubes of 2 in. o.d. and 14 flues of $5\frac{1}{8}$ in. o.d., which are 15 ft. $2\frac{1}{2}$ in. long. Each flue houses 6 elements of 1 in. o.d. The inside firebox has a length of 8 ft. $2\frac{1}{2}$ in., a maximum depth of 6 ft. 6 in., and a width at the grate of 3 ft. $2\frac{1}{2}$ in. The whistle has the common G.W.R. curved plate shield between it and the cab.

Cylinders of $18\frac{1}{2}$ in. diameter by 30 in. stroke have been fitted since 1907, compared with 18 in. by 30 in. for the original engines; the weight now is 75.5 tons against 68.3 tons, and the maximum axle load 17.25 tons against 16.35 tons. At 75 per cent. of the boiler pressure the tractive effort is 31,200 lb. and the factor of adhesion 4.85 against the weight of 67.5 tons. Stephenson's link motion is used to operate the piston valves. The tender is of the usual 3,500-gal. type weighing 40 tons full, whereas the original tenders were of 3,000-gal. capacity and weighed 36.75 tons. The present engine plus tender weight is thus 115.5 tons. The single-window cab locomotives weigh 76.25 tons. These engines are considered capable of negotiating curves of 6 chains radius at dead slow speed.

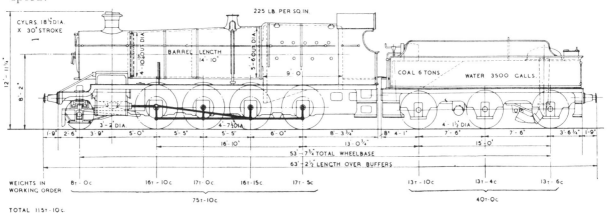

2-8-0 MIXED-TRAFFIC LOCOMOTIVE, G.W.R.

ONE of Mr. Churchward's last main line designs was a large 2-8-0 engine for mixed traffic service which was built in 1919. This machine, No. 4700, had 5 ft. 8 in. wheels; in 1921 it was given a much larger boiler which increased the total weight by 4.3 tons, the maximum axle load by 1.8 tons, and the heating surface by 390 sq. ft., and since that time eight further engines to the large boiler design (but with different superheaters) have been built at Swindon, and are illustrated by the accompanying photograph and diagram. They are used principally on express goods trains, but passenger braking and heating equipment is fitted.

A taper boiler is fitted, of course, but is not standard with any other Great Western class. The firebox is almost the same as those fitted to the 4-6-0 Castle class, and the barrel is akin to that of the King class, but is shorter and has not the same arrangement of tubes. The barrel is 14 ft. 10 in. long and tapers from 6 ft. o.d. at the back to 5 ft. 6 in. at the front. It contains 218 tubes of 2 in. o.d. and 16 flues of $5\frac{1}{8}$ in. o.d. which give a heating surface of 2,062 sq. ft. The firebox, with a maximum length inside of 9 ft. $2\frac{1}{2}$ in. contributes 170 sq. ft. to the total evaporative surface of 2,232 sq. ft. The length between tubeplates is 15 ft. $2\frac{1}{2}$ in. The superheating surface of the Swindon small element (1.0 in. o.d.) superheater is 290 sq. ft. The superheating surface of the 1921 design of big boiler was 324 sq. ft. The grate area is 30.3 sq. ft., and the boiler works at the standard G.W.R. pressure of 225 lb. per sq. in.

The two 19 in. by 30 in. outside cylinders have overhead piston valves driven by inside Stephenson link motion. As is usual in G.W.R. practice the cylinders are horizontal but with the centre lines 2 in. above the wheel centres when the engine is new. The spring rigging on each side is compensated in two groups. At 75 per cent of the boiler pressure the tractive effort is 26,900 lb., giving a factor of adhesion of 6.1 against the adhesion weight of 73.4 tons. Added to the engine weight of 82 tons is the 40 tons of the 3,500-gal. tender, giving a total of 122 tons. The tender carries 5 tons of coal, and, like the engine, is braked on the vacuum system. Tenders of 4,000 gal. capacity and weighing 46.7 tons are used now.

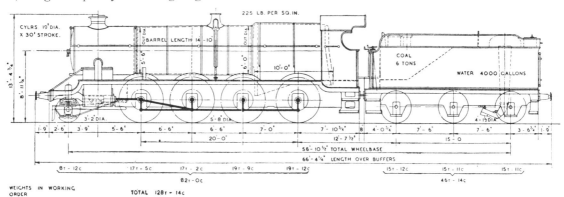

2-8-2T FREIGHT LOCOMOTIVE, G.W.R.

NUMEROUS two-cylinder 2-8-0 tank engines were built before and after the 1914-18 war by the Great Western Railway for short-distance mineral traffic, principally in South Wales, and were classed as 4200 and 5200. They weighed 82.1 tons and were 40 ft. 9 in. long over buffers. Owing to the falling off in the coal export trade of South Wales, many of these engines were not required in that district, and beginning in 1934 conversions were made to the 2-8-2T type, and the rebuilt locomotives are being used on the slow main line trains, replacing in some instances the old Aberdare outside-framed 2-6-0 class.

The conversion has been cleverly carried out, and very little alteration has been necessary. The bunker and rear water tank have been lengthened, a piece lapped on to the main frames beneath, and a trailing radial truck added. This truck is of the G.W.R.'s standard pattern, but has increased sideplay. The boiler, smokebox, cylinders, valve gear, wheels and motion are the same, but the weight has been increased by 10.5 tons and the length by 4 ft. 1 in. The boiler is the same as that used in the 3100 class of 2-6-2T and the 4300 class of single-window cab 2-6-0 engine.

One of the standard types of taper boiler is fitted and the 14 flues of $5\frac{1}{8}$ in. o.d. and 235 tubes of $1\frac{5}{8}$ in. diameter provide 1,350 sq. ft. of heating surface. To this must be added the 129 sq. ft. from the Belpaire firebox, giving an evaporative total of 1,479 sq. ft. The superheater is of the low-temperature type favoured at Swindon and the six 1 in. element tubes in each of the 14 flues give an aggregate surface of 192 sq. ft. The grate area is 20.5 sq. ft. The boiler barrel tapers from 5 ft. 6 in. o.d. at the throat plate to 4ft. $10\frac{3}{4}$ in. o.d. at the front, and the distance between tubeplates is 11 ft. $4\frac{1}{2}$ in.

The two outside cylinders are 19 in. by 30 in. and have overhead piston valves actuated by Stephenson link motion between the frames, the drive being taken through rocking shafts. The cylinders drive the second pair of 4 ft. $7\frac{1}{2}$ in. coupled wheels. At 75 per cent. of the boiler pressure of 200 lb. the tractive effort is 29,300 lb., giving a factor of 5.5 against the adhesion weight of 72.75 tons.

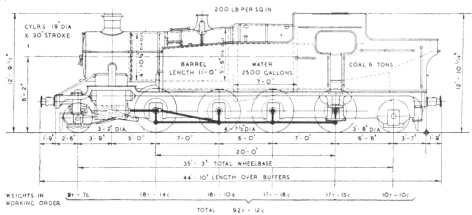

2-6-2T LOCOMOTIVES, G.W.R.

THE most numerous of the larger types of 2-6-2 tank engines on the Great Western Railway are the 51XX and 61XX classes with 5 ft. 8 in. coupled wheels. Apart from boiler pressure they are almost identical. The numbers run from 5100 to 5189 and from 6100 to 6129, the former series originating in 1929 and the second in 1931.

The boiler of the 51XX class is a duplicate of those fitted to the 66XX 0-6-2 tanks, and works at 200 lb. pressure, but in the 61XX series thicker plates are used and the pressure is 225 lb. per sq. in. The heating surface is 1,145 sq. ft., the firebox surface 122 sq. ft., the total evaporative surface 1,267 sq. ft., and the grate area 20.3 sq. ft. There are 28 tubes of $1\frac{5}{8}$ in. o.d. and six flues of $5\frac{1}{8}$ in. o.d., 11 ft. $4\frac{1}{4}$ in. long. The superheating surface is 82 sq. ft.

Two 18 in. by 30 in. outside cylinders drive the second pair of 5 ft. 8 in. coupled wheels. They have overhead piston valves actuated through rocking shafts by Stephenson's link motion between the frames, and outside steam pipes from the superheater header. The running plate at the forward end of the tanks is strengthened to support the slide bar support bracket, a convenient location for which could not be found between the wheels. The helical springs of the pony truck are equalised with the laminated springs of the leading coupled wheels. The remaining springs are independent.

At 75 per cent. of the boiler pressure the tractive effort of the 61XX series is 24,100 lb., giving a factor of 4.9 against the adhesion weight of 52.65 tons when the tanks are holding 2,000 gallons of water. With the same assumption the tractive effort of the 51XX class is 21,400 lb. and the factor of adhesion 5.3.

In 1939 some 2-6-2T engines were built at Swindon and classified 31XX and 81XX. The latter are virtually duplicates of the 61XX series, but weigh 76.5 tons. The former, shown in the diagram on this page, have $18\frac{1}{2}$ in. by 30 in. cylinders, 5 ft. 3 in. wheels, 225 lb. pressure, 235 tubes of $1\frac{5}{8}$ in. o.d. and 14 flues of $5\frac{1}{8}$ in. o.d., an evaporative surface of 1,478 sq. ft., of which 129 sq. ft. comes from the firebox, a grate area of 20.5 sq. ft., a tank capacity of 2,000 gal., and a coal capacity of $3\frac{1}{2}$ tons. These are the largest and heaviest of the G.W.R. 2-6-2T engines.

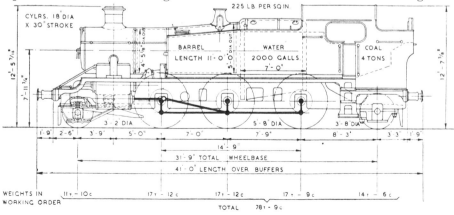

0-6-0PT LOCOMOTIVES, G.W.R.

WHAT may be regarded as the standard Great Western shunting locomotive is the 57XX type of pannier tank, an inside-cylinder parallel domed boiler locomotive. There are now 400 of these locomotives, Nos. 5700-5799, 6700-6749, 7700-7799, 8700-8749 and 9700-9799, of which 9700-09 are combined side and pannier tanks and have condensing gear.

The boiler has a maximum external diameter of 4 ft. 5 in. and the barrel is 10 ft. 3 in. long; it is constructed of $\frac{9}{16}$ in. plates. Although not fitted with a superheater, the barrel has two $5\frac{1}{8}$ in. diameter flues in addition to the 219 tubes of $1\frac{5}{8}$ in. diameter. Tubes and flues together provide a heating surface of 1,013 sq. ft. The distance between tubeplates is 10 ft. $6\frac{3}{4}$ in. A Belpaire firebox of the raised pattern is used; it is 5 ft. 4 in. long outside and 4 ft. wide at the foundation ring; the grate is horizontal and the total depth of the outside box is 6 ft. The inside copper box has a heating surface of 102 sq. ft., and the total evaporative surface is 1,115 sq. ft. A safety valve on top of the firebox limits the working pressure to 200 lb. per sq. in., and the grate has an area of 15.3 sq. ft.

To clear the leading axle the two $17\frac{1}{2}$ in. by 24 in. inside cylinders are set at a relatively steep angle; they are fitted with slide valves actuated by Stephenson link motion. The wheels are 4 ft. $7\frac{1}{2}$ in. diameter. Underhung laminated springs take the weight on the two leading axles, but overhung volute springs are used for the trailing boxes. At 75 per cent. of the working pressure the tractive effort is 19,800 lb. This gives a factor of adhesion of 5.4 with tanks and bunker full and about 4.7 when empty. The tank capacity is 1,200 gal. and the bunker holds $3\frac{1}{4}$ tons of coal. In full working order the locomotive scales 47.5 tons, and has a maximum axle load of 16.75 tons, but in certain batches the weight has been increased to 49 tons and the axle load to 17 tons.

Other Great Western 0-6-0 pannier, or wing tank engines are the 5400 class, with 5 ft. 2 in. wheels, 14 ft. 8 in. wheelbase, 1,086 sq. ft. of heating surface, $16\frac{3}{4}$ sq. ft. of grate area, $16\frac{1}{2}$ in. by 24 in. cylinders, and 46.6 tons weight.

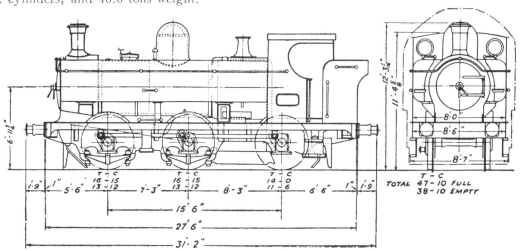

4-6-2 STREAMLINED LOCOMOTIVE, S.R.

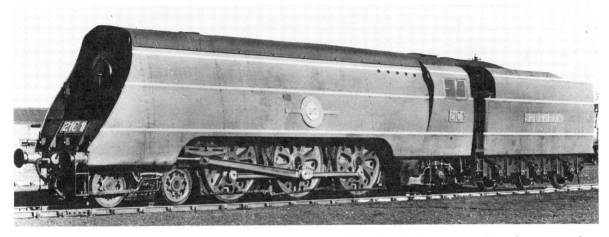

THE long-awaited Southern Railway Pacifics were introduced early in 1941, and one by one as they came out of Eastleigh works the first ten were named after well-known shipping lines. Designed under the responsibility of Mr. O. V. S. Bulleid, these locomotives exhibit many unusual features, in addition to being semi-streamlined. They have box, or double-disc type coupled wheel centres; three cylinders with valves operated by the designer's patent radial chain-driven valve motion; two thermic syphons; welded steel fireboxes; and a complete electric lighting installation. In general, they work passenger and freight trains over the West of England line between London and Exeter, and in ordinary service have shown a good turn of speed despite the relatively small coupled wheels, 85-90 m.p.h. being reached down the short, steep banks between Salisbury and Exeter.

A boiler pressure of 280 lb.—the highest in England—is used. The boiler barrel is of tapered form, but has the taper on the bottom side only. Maximum and minimum outside diameters are 6 ft. $3\frac{1}{2}$ in. and 5 ft. $9\frac{3}{4}$ in. The 124 tubes are $2\frac{1}{4}$ in. o.d. and 40 flues $5\frac{1}{4}$ in. o.d., and 17 ft. long; they give a heating surface of 2,176 sq. ft., and the firebox (with combustion chamber) an additional 275 sq. ft. including syphons, making a total evaporative surface of 2,451 sq. ft. A superheating surface of 822 sq. ft. is provided, and the grate area of the wide firebox is $48\frac{1}{2}$ sq. ft. Spun-glass mattresses are used for the boiler lagging; the firehole doors are steam-operated.

All three 18 in. cylinders drive the centre coupled axle, and in their short stroke of 24 in. are reminiscent of H. A. Ivatt and his celebrated Atlantics. The inside cylinder is set at the very steep inclination of 1 in $7\frac{1}{2}$, but the outside pair are nearly horizontal. At 75 per cent. of the boiler pressure the tractive effort is 33,100 lb., corresponding to a factor of adhesion of 4.2 against the 63 tons on the coupled wheels. All three sets of valve motion are enclosed in an oil-tight casing between the frames, and this casing also encloses the centre connecting rod, crosshead and crank. The reversing gear is power-operated by steam and hydraulic cylinders. The 6 ft. 2 in. coupled wheels, and also the tender wheels, have clasp rigging for the brake blocks.

Like the streamlined casing and cab, the tender superstructure is of welded steel, and the tank is filled through holes in the tender cab end.

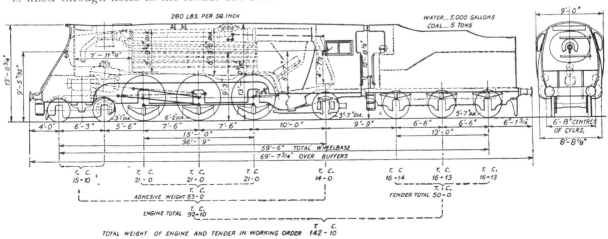

4-6-0 LORD NELSON LOCOMOTIVE, S.R.

INTENDED principally for the efficient operation of the heavy West of England trains, the Lord Nelson 4-6-0 engines were built at Eastlegh works in 1926-9, and the first batch was fitted with bogie tenders weighing 56.7 tons and holding 5,000 gal. of water. In 1928 some of the engines were provided with six-wheeled tenders holding 4,500 gal. of water and 5 tons of coal, for use on the Dover boat trains, where the bigger tenders are not required.

A parallel boiler with a minimum internal diameter of 5 ft. $6\frac{1}{8}$ in. is used, the plates being $\frac{23}{32}$ in. thick. There are 173 tubes of 2 in. o.d. and 27 flues of $5\frac{1}{4}$ in. o.d., 14 ft. 2 in. long, which give a heating surface of 1,795 sq. ft. The firebox heating surface is 194 sq. ft., and the total evaporative surface 1,989 sq. ft. The firebox is of the Belpaire type with well-radiused plates and rigid roof staying reminiscent of G.W.R. practice. The grate has an area of 33 sq. ft. and the firebox a volume of about 208 cu. ft. The superheater has a header of the Maunsell type and the 27 elements of $1\frac{3}{8}$ in. o.d. provide a surface of 376 sq. ft. One of the engines has been fitted with a boiler 10 in. longer than the normal, giving a tube heating surface of 1,902 sq. ft., and about 1939 a beginning was made with the provision of improved exhaust arrangements involving the use of a double chimney, and all engines of this type now have a Lemaitre blast pipe and a wide chimney.

The most striking mechanical feature of the Lord Nelson class is the adoption of the 135° crank arrangement, the two cylinders at each side being arranged at 135° to each other and at 90° to those on the other side, this giving eight unequally spaced exhaust beats per revolution. The two inside cylinders drive a built-up crank axle between the two front coupled wheels and the outside pair drive the centre coupled wheels through connecting rods 11 ft. long. The steam events are controlled by 8 in. piston valves driven by independent sets of Walschaerts gear, but the two inside sets are driven by a common eccentric and eccentric rod. One engine, No. 859 *Lord Hood*, was provided with 6 ft. 3 in. coupled wheels. No side draft plates were fitted originally.

At 75 per cent. of the boiler pressure of 220 lb. per sq. in. the four $16\frac{1}{2}$ by 26 in. cylinders produce a tractive effort of 29,550 lb. at the rims of the 6 ft. 7 in. driving wheels, giving a factor of adhesion of 4.7 against the adhesion weight of 61.95 tons. The locomotive weighs 83.5 tons in working order, and with the bogie tender 140.2 tons. With a six-wheeled tender the aggregate weight is 130 tons.

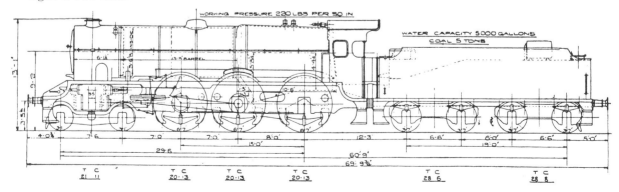

4-6-0 KING ARTHUR LOCOMOTIVE, S.R.

THE King Arthur six-coupled class was derived directly from the 736 class of 4-6-0 engine introduced by Mr. Urie on the L.S.W.R. in the year 1917, but the 22 in. by 28 in. cylinders of those locomotives were reduced to 20½ in. by 28 in. in the King Arthurs, and the boiler pressure raised from 180 to 200 lb. per sq. in. Actually the Urie engines have now been rebuilt as King Arthurs, and new engines to the modified design were built by the North British Locomotive Co., Ltd. As with the Lord Nelson class, some of the engines have six-wheeled tenders and are used on the Eastern section, whereas those used on the Western section have double-bogie tenders of 5,000 gal. capacity and weighing 57.55 tons. Six or more of the class have been fitted with Lemaitre multiple-jet blast pipes, and one so fitted is shown above.

A slightly taper boiler is used, the taper being all in the front ring, which is reduced from 5 ft. 3 in. to 5 ft. 0 in. inside diameter. The barrel is 13 ft. 9 in. long and the distance between tubeplates is 14 ft. 2 in. A heating surface of 1,716 sq. ft. is provided by the 167 tubes of 2 in. o.d. and the 24 flues of 5¼ in. o.d. The evaporative total of 1,878 sq. ft. is made up by the addition of 162 sq. ft. from the firebox. The round-topped firebox has a length inside at the bottom of 8 ft. 5½ in. and a width of 3 ft. 6¼ in. at the grate, this relatively great width being due to the narrow water space, 2 in., above the foundation ring. The grate area is 30 sq. ft., and the superheating surface 337 sq. ft.

The two cylinders are set at an inclination of 1 in 110 and the steam events are controlled by 11 in. piston valves with a maximum travel of 6⅜ in. A tractive effort of 22,400 lb. is produced at 75 per cent. of the working pressure of 200 lb. per sq. in. giving the high factor of adhesion of 6.0 against the adhesion weight of 60 tons. The total engine weight is 80.95 tons and the engine plus tender weight 138.5 tons with the bogie tender. The coupled wheels are braked by means of a 24-in. vacuum cylinder to about 50 per cent. of the weight resting on them. The long bogie wheelbase is in a way a relic of the days of Wm. Adams, and was resuscitated by Robert Urie after Dugald Drummond had gone back to the more usual 6 ft. 6 in.

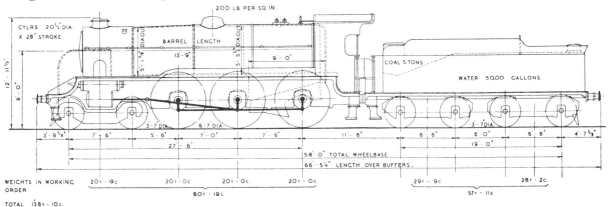

4-4-0 SCHOOLS CLASS LOCOMOTIVE, S.R.

NAMED after famous public schools on the Southern Railway system, ten large 3-cylinder 4-4-0 locomotives for express work were built at Eastleigh in 1930, and since that date another 30 have been set to work. They have been used mainly on the Eastern and Western sections, and do splendid work on such routes as that from Charing Cross to Hastings with trains of 350-360 tons weight. For some years they have operated heavy trains most successfully on the London-Southampton-Bournemouth route. It was claimed by the Southern that they are the most powerful engines of their wheel arrangement in Europe. The bogie, individual sets of motion, springs and other details are similar to those of the four-cylinder Lord Nelson 4-6-0s, and the firebox is similar to that of the King Arthur class, but has a slightly smaller grate area. A round-top firebox was fitted for reasons of weight, and the maximum dimensions pass th smallest Southern loading gauge.

The parallel boiler has a minimum inside diameter of 5 ft. 3 in. and a length between tube-plates of 12 ft. 3½ in. It contains 216 tubes of 1¼ in. o.d. and 24 flues of 5¼ in. o.d. which together give 1,604 sq. ft. of heating surface. The firebox contributes 162 sq. ft. to the total evaporative surface of 1,766 sq. ft., and the superheater, with a Maunsell type header and elements of 1⅜/1³⁄₃₂ in. diameter, provides a surface of 283 sq. ft. The grate area is 28.3 sq. ft., and on top of the firebox are two 3 in. Ross pop safety valves. Wide-chimney exhaust with Lemaitre blast pipe arrangements are now fitted to about a score of the class.

Each of the three 16½ in. by 26 in. cylinders has its own 8-in. piston valve and independent set of Walschaerts gear. The exhaust passages are extremely short and direct and terminate in a 5-in. blast pipe nozzle. The slide bars are carried in centre supports in the usual Southern fashion. At 75 per cent. of the boiler pressure the tractive effort is 22,200 lb. giving a factor of 4.2 against the adhesion weight of 42 tons. The total weight of the engine is 67.1 tons, or 109.5 tons with the six-wheeled tender.

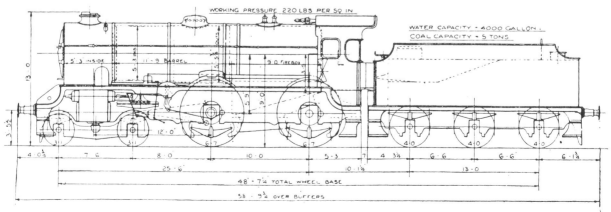

2-6-0 LOCOMOTIVES, S.R.

FROM the 2-6-0 two-cylinder mixed traffic locomotive No. 810 built by the S.E.C.R. in 1917 was developed the long line of two-cylinder and three-cylinder mixed traffic engines of the Southern Railway, but it was not until the beginning of 1929 that the design was modified for passenger service by the provision of 6 ft. wheels in place of the 5 ft. 6 in. of the mixed traffic locomotives. In that year 10 Class U two-cylinder engines were built at Brighton and 10 at Ashford.

The cylinders, motion, valve gear and boilers are identical with those of the N class fast freight engines. The boiler is of the taper type with a maximum barrel diameter of 5 ft. 3 in. at the firebox and a minimum diameter of 4 ft. 8 in. at the front. The 173 tubes of 1¾ in. o.d. and the 21 flues of 5⅛ in. o.d. produce a heating surface of 1,391 sq. ft., and the Belpaire firebox contributes 135 sq. ft. to the total of 1,526 sq. ft. The grate area is 25 sq. ft. and the superheating surface is 285 sq. ft. It is worth noting that all of these dimensions except the superheating surface had remained unchanged since the first mixed traffic Mogul was built at Ashford in 1917.

The two 19 in. by 28 in. cylinders have 10 in. piston valves with a maximum travel of about 6½ in. The maximum tractive effort is 21,000 lb., assuming 75 per cent. of the boiler pressure; related to the adhesion weight of 53.5 tons this gives an adhesion factor of 5.7. The leading Bissel truck has Cartazzi slides and carries only 8.8 tons, and the total locomotive weight is 62.3 tons; the empty weight is 57.4 tons. The tender is of one of the Southern's standard patterns, and carries 5 tons of coal and 3,500 gal. of water on an all-in weight of 40.5 tons. In full working order the engine plus tender weight is 102.8 tons. The later engines have 42½-ton, 4,000-gal. tenders.

The U1 class has three 16 in. by 28 in. cylinders, weighs 65.3 tons, and has a tractive effort at 75 per cent. of the boiler pressure of 22,450 lb., giving a factor of 5.45 against the adhesion weight of 54.7 tons. There are corresponding two-cylinder and three-cylinder mixed-traffic versions of these engines, classified N and N1, which have 5 ft. 6 in. wheels and slightly lower total weights of 61.2 and 64.25 tons respectively, and a dhesion totals of 52.2 and 53.75 tons.

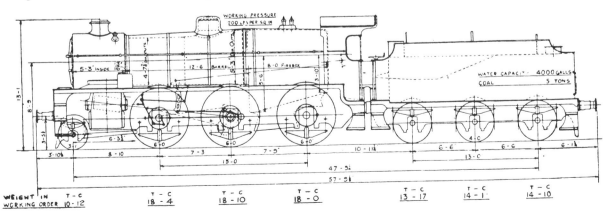

4-6-0 MIXED-TRAFFIC LOCOMOTIVE, S.R.

JUST after 1918 a series of 4-6-0 engines for fast freight service were built by the L. & S.W.R., and were small-wheeled counterparts of Mr. Urie's 4-6-0 express engines of the 736 class, which after the 1923 railway amalgamation were developed into the well-known King Arthur class. A similar development took place with the freight locomotives, which, with many King Arthur characteristics, were built up to 1927, and used on fast goods and passenger excursion trains. Originally, there were 20 engines built in 1920 for the L.S.W.R. under Mr. Urie's direction; and another 15 to a modified design were built for the Southern Railway at Eastleigh in 1927 to the requirements of Mr. Maunsell.

A new batch of these engines, classified as S.15, was built at Eastleigh in 1936, and are cut down in height and width so that they may work over the Eastern section of the Southern Railway. The last five of the ten engines of 1936 have six-wheeled tenders with a water capacity of 4,000 gallons, which were taken from certain engines of the King Arthur class and replaced by the new double-bogie 5,000 gallon tenders. In these engines the length over buffers is reduced to 61 ft. 3 in. and the total wheelbase to 51 ft. 3¾ in. instead of the figures given on the accompanying diagram of the bogie tender design. The adhesion weight is 59.25 tons, the engine weight 79.25 tons, and the total for the engine and tender 135.65 tons. The load over the coupled axles is very evenly distributed, varying only between 19½ and 20 tons. The connecting-rod big-ends are unusual in modern practice in being of the double-bolt strap type.

The two 20½ in. by 28 in. cylinders have 11 in. piston valves with a maximum travel of 6⅜ in. With 75 per cent. of the boiler pressure they provide a maximum tractive effort at the wheel rims of 26,350 lb., giving a factor of adhesion of 5.0. The boiler is identical with those of the King Arthur class and contains 24 flues of 5¼ in. o.d and 167 tubes of 2 in. o.d., which together give a heating surface of 1,716 sq. ft.; the firebox accounts for 162 sq. ft., and the total evaporative surface thus is 1,878 sq. ft. The grate area of the round-topped firebox is 28 sq. ft., and super-heater has a surface of 337 sq. ft. Vacuum brakes are fitted to both engine and tender, one 30-in. cylinder on each applying the brake power. As usual on the locomotives of the Southern Railway, the small ejector is replaced by a pump driven from the left-hand crosshead. The double-bogie tenders have straight-sided tanks of electrically-welded construction, and the bogies incorporate disc wheels. The forward part of the fuel bunker is of the self-trimming type. No water pick-up gear is fitted to these or any other tenders on the same railway, for the Southern has no water troughs.

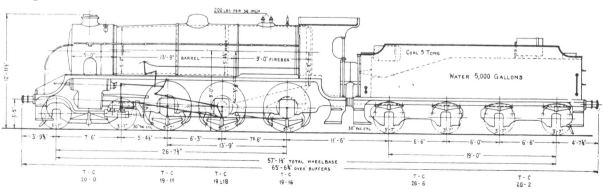

0-6-0 MAUNSELL FREIGHT LOCOMOTIVE, S.R.

SHORTLY before his retirement, Mr. R. E. L. Maunsell designed a class of 0-6-0 general freight engines which were the first of that wheel arrangement to be built for the Southern Railway. There are twenty of these engines in all, classified as Q in the Southern list, and numbered 530-49, but none were actually delivered until Mr. Maunsell had been succeeded as C.M.E. by Mr. Bulleid. They were constructed at Eastleigh and are fitted with vacuum brakes and steam heating connections so that passenger trains and braked freight trains can be handled. Vacuum brakes also operate the engine and tender blocks.

The boiler is very slightly tapered, from 4 ft. 7⅞ in. outside diameter at the front to 5 ft. at the back, in a length of 10 ft. 9½ in. It is fitted with a Belpaire firebox and a raised type of extended smokebox. There are 158 tubes of 1¾ in. o.d. and 21 flues of 5¼ in. o.d. and 11 ft. 2¼ in. long; these give respective heating surfaces of 810 and 315 sq. ft., and the firebox contributes 122 sq. ft. to the evaporative total of 1,247 sq. ft. A Sinuflo superheater is fitted, and the 21 elements give a surface of 185 sq. ft. Apart from *Lord Howe*, one of the Lord Nelson class of 4-6-0, these are the only engines on the Southern to be equipped with this pattern of element. A sloping grate with an area of 21.9 sq. ft. is provided, and on top of it are provided two Ross pop safety valves set to relieve the pressure at 200 lb. per sq. in.

Two 19 in. by 26 in. inside cylinders drive a solid crank axle. Above them are long-travel piston valves 10 in. diameter, operated through rocking levers by Stephenson link motion. Steam reversing gear with horizontal cylinders is fitted on the left-hand side of the engine. The driving axleboxes are supported by underhung helical steel springs and the coupled boxes by laminated springs. The arrangement of the sanding gear is worth mention. Steam sanders are placed before the leading coupled wheels and behind the driving wheels, and behind the trailing coupled wheels there is a de-sander or rail washer, from which a jet of hot water issues to wash the sand off the rails when running forward. This feature is to ensure that the operation of track circuits is not impeded by sand remaining on the rails after use.

A Southern Railway standard 3,500 gal. tender is fitted, and the total weight of engine and tender is 90 tons fully laden and 65¾ tons empty. The maximum axle load is the moderate figure of 18 tons, and the distribution of the locomotive weight is, perhaps, unusual, as may be seen from the diagram. Nevertheless, it is on basically sound principles, as when running forward the draw-bar reaction tends to increase the weight on the trailing wheels. At 75 per cent. of the working pressure the tractive effort is 23,100 lb., which gives a factor of adhesion of 4.8 against the engine weight of 49½ tons. The maximum overall width of the combined engine and tender is only 8 ft. 4 in.

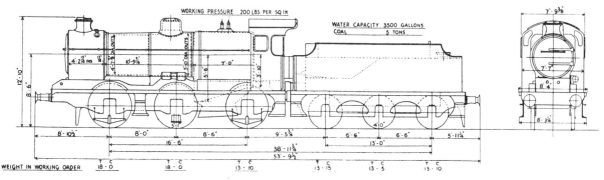

0-6-0 FREIGHT LOCOMOTIVE, S.R.

THE Bulleid 0-6-0 freight engines of class Q1 were introduced early in 1942, and exhibit nearly as many novel features as the Merchant Navy Pacifics, but of course some of these features were influenced by war-time conditions. The most notable superficial feature is the absence of running plates and the method of carrying the boiler cleading sheets, and these draw even greater attention to the box-form double-disc wheels.

In providing the largest practicable boiler capacity it was found expedient to use the same firebox throat and back plate flanging blocks as used for the Lord Nelson engines. The boiler barrel is tapered equally on top and bottom from 5 ft. to 5 ft. 9 in. outside; within the barrel are 209 tubes of $1\frac{3}{4}$ in. o.d. and 21 flues $5\frac{1}{8}$ in. o.dd., 10 ft. 6 in. long, which together give 1,472 sq. ft. of heating surface. The firebox heating surface of 170 sq. ft.—a notable contribution for an 0-6-0 locomotive—raises the evaporative total to 1,642 sq. ft. The superheating surface is 218 sq. ft. and the grate area 27 sq. ft. The complete boiler proportions should give quick and excellent steam-raising capacity, though with a high gas temperature in the smokebox, as is only natural with the short tube length. Monel metal firebox side stays in the breaking zones and spun-glass lagging are other features of the boiler. The steel clothing plates are supported by the main frame.

Two inside cylinders 19 in. diameter by 26 in. stroke drive the centre pair of 61 in. wheels, and their outside-admission piston valves are operated by Stephenson link motion giving a maximum travel of $6\frac{7}{8}$ in. The blast pipe has a five-jet nozzle. The cast steel box wheels are of the same B.F.B. patent type as in the Merchant Navy 4-6-2 engines. The tender has a welded steel tank and a self-trimming coal bunker. At 75 per cent. of the boiler pressure the tractive effort at the wheel rims is 26,500 lb., giving an adhesive factor of 4.35. Train brake and heating equipment is fitted.

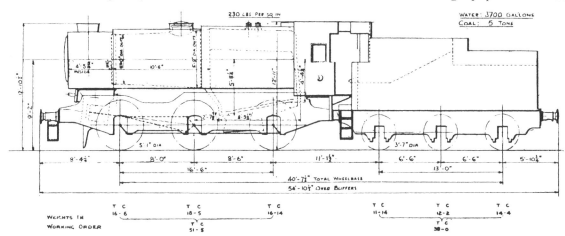

2-6-4T FREIGHT LOCOMOTIVE, S.R.

AFTER the Sevenoaks derailment in 1927, involving one of the River class passenger tank engines, no steam engines without tenders for anything but yard service were set to work on the Southern Railway until 1932, when the first of a series of 15 locomotives of the 2-6-4T wheel arrangement was completed. Known as Class W in the Southern list, five of these engines were built at Eastleigh and ten at Ashford. Although of the same wheel arrangement as the River class tanks, the W class locomotives—used mainly for short-distance goods traffic—have a different suspension arrangement and method of control for the bogie and pony truck. Of the three-cylinder type, they embody many of the details of the N1 class of Mogul tender engines, and have the same size of wheel, viz., 5 ft. 6 in.

The boiler is of the taper type, the back ring having a maximum external diameter of 5 ft. 3 in., and the front ring being parallel with an outside diameter of 4 ft. 8 in. The heating surface of the tubes and flues amounts to 1,391 sq. ft. and that of the tapered Belpaire firebox to 135 sq. ft., giving an evaporative total of 1,526 sq. ft. The boiler barrel houses 173 tubes of $1\frac{3}{4}$ in. o.d. and 21 flues of $5\frac{1}{8}$ in. o.d., and with a length of 12 ft. $10\frac{3}{4}$ in. The superheater, with a Maunsell header, has a surface of 285 sq. ft., and the steeply-sloping grate has an area of 25 sq. ft. Two Ross pop safety valves limit the pressur to 200 lb. per sq. in.

All three $16\frac{1}{2}$ in. by 28 in. cylinders drive the centre coupled axle. Only two outside sets of Walschaerts gear are utilised, the motion of the inside valve being derived from cross rods worked from the tops of the combination levers of the outside gears. At 75 per cent. of the working pressure a tractive effort of 26,000 lb. is obtained, resulting in a factor of adhesion of 4.9 with full tanks. Of the total working order weight of 90.7 tons, 63 per cent. ranks as adhesive. The side and rear tanks hold an aggregate of 2,000 gal. of water and the bunker capacity is equivalent to $3\frac{1}{2}$ tons of coal. A powerful graduated steam brake is fitted, and works in conjunction with the train vacuum apparatus on braked stock. Blocks are applied to all coupled and bogie wheels.

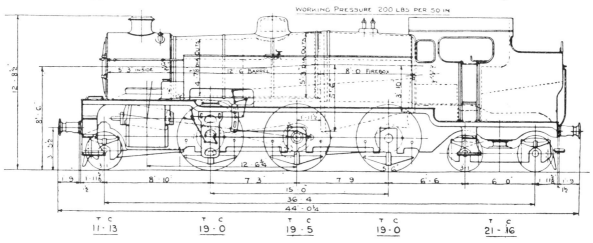

0-8-0T SHUNTING LOCOMOTIVE, S.R.

FOR service in the principal goods yards and sorting sidings, and in the various hump yards, eight three-cylinder 0-8-0 tanks were built at Brighton in 1929-30. They form the only eight-coupled design built since the Southern Railway came into being in 1923, and the only other eight-coupled class is the 4-8-0T design built for the same type of service by the L. & S.W.R. in 1921. The Brighton-built tanks are used at such places as Hither Green sidings, Salisbury and Exeter. The leading and trailing wheels are provided with sideplay so that curves of 300 ft. radius can be taken despite a wheelbase of 17 ft. 6 in., but the overhang of almost 11 ft. at each end is very long, so that the sharp curves might be negotiated only where space was ample.

No superheater is fitted, in view of the nature of the work to be performed. The parallel boiler barrel has a maximum outside diameter of 5 ft. and contains 242 tubes of $1\frac{3}{4}$ in. o.d. and 10 ft. 7 in. long, which give a heating surface of 1,173 sq. ft. The grate and firebox have been kept small in order to minimise stand-by losses; the firebox heating surface of 106 sq. ft. brings the total evaporative surface up to 1,279 sq. ft. The grate area is 18.6 sq. ft.

The cylinders have a diameter of 16 in. and a stroke of 28 in. The outside pair drive the third axle through 11 ft. 6 in. connecting rods, and the inside cylinder, set at an inclination of 1 in 8, drives the second axle. Walschaerts' gear controls the outside piston valves, but for the inside valve one of J. T. Marshall's gears is used, in which a second eccentric provides the lap and lead movement usually derived from the crosshead in Walschaerts gear. Reversing is by steam.

The tractive effort at 75% of the working pressure amounts to 25,900 lb. giving a factor of adhesion of 6.2 against the full working order weight of 71.6 tons. Steam brakes are used, but vacuum apparatus is fitted to enable braked trains to be handled, and a steam heating cock and pipes are incorporated so that the engines can perform pilot duties with passenger trains.

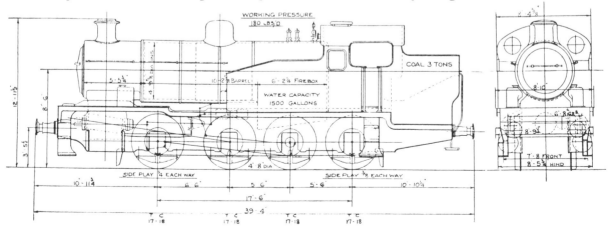

2-8-0 AMERICAN LOCOMOTIVE, M. OF SUPPLY

IN order to cope with the greatly increased freight traffics of British railways owing to war conditions and to the presence of so many American troops, the Ministry of Supply in 1942 placed orders for many 2-8-0 locomotives, and to expedite delivery some of the orders were placed in America and general constructional details left in the hands of the builders on the other side of the Atlantic. The first shipment of these American-built engines arrived towards the end of 1942, and emanated from the works of the American Locomotive Company. As with the British-built Ministry of Supply Consolidations, these locomotives have been designed on a basis of simplicity and of economy in labour and in certain constructional materials.

The parallel two-ring boiler barrel has a maximum external diameter of 5 ft. 10 in., and though the smokebox tubeplate is of the drumhead type, the lagging plates are "swaged" down at the front to prevent an unsightly step down in diameter between lagging plates and smokebox plates. On top of the barrel, the dome and two sandboxes are covered by a common casing, and just behind this, on the back ring, are two pop safety valves. The smokebox and offset smokebox door design and proportions are in accordance with American practice, and the Westinghouse brake pump is carried on the smokebox front plate and thus does not interfere with the look-out from the cab. The barrel contains 150 steel tubes of 2 in. o.d. and 30 flues of $5\frac{3}{8}$ in. o.d., 13 ft. 5 in. long; together with the surface provided by the steel inner firebox they give a total heating surface of 1,773 sq. ft.; the superheater has a surface of 480 sq. ft. The round-topped, wide firebox has a grate 7 ft. long by 5 ft. 10 in. wide with an area of 41 sq. ft., this being a considerable increase over the grate area of the British-built 2-8-0 engines with narrow fireboxes.

At 75 per cent. of the working pressure of 225 lb. per sq. in. the two outside 19 in. by 26 in. cylinders exert a tractive effort of 28,000 lb. at the rims of the 57 in. wheels, and this gives a factor of adhesion of 5.0 against the $62\frac{1}{2}$ tons on the coupled wheels. The coupled axle journals are all 8 in. diameter by 11 in. long. Walschaerts valve motion gives a maximum travel of $6\frac{1}{2}$ in. to the overhead piston valves, and the corresponding lap and lead are $1\frac{1}{4}$ in. and $\frac{1}{4}$ in. The steam pipes are very direct. The total engine weight is 72/73 tons, and with a full complement of 8 tons of coal and 5,500 gal. of water the engine and double-bogie tender scale 124/125 tons. The locomotive is built up on bar frames, and the springing is compensated into a three-point suspension system. Steam brakes apply blocks on all the coupled wheels, and both Westinghouse and vacuum equipment is incorporated for the application of train brakes.

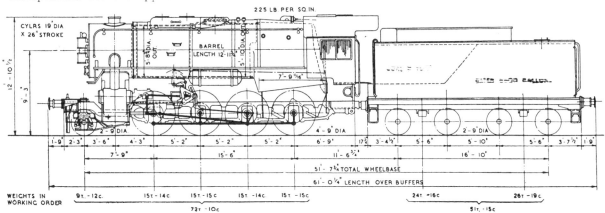

2-8-0 M. OF SUPPLY (BRITISH-BUILT) LOCOMOTIVE

AFTER experience with and consideration of the W.D. 2-8-0 locomotives ordered in 1939 for shipment to France and elsewhere overseas, and the American-built 2-8-0 engines, the Ministry of Supply 2-8-0 locomotives which were introduced early in 1943 were based on the Stanier 2-8-0 engines, and thus are not unlike the W.D. engines of 1939-40, major differences being ½ in. increase in the cylinder diameter and an eight-wheel tender holding 1,000 gal. more water than the six-wheel pattern of the W.D. units. The intention was to have a design which could be built by several British builders and works, and which would involve only materials readily available, and also to have simplicity of design. As far as possible, renewable parts are duplicates of those of the L.M.S.R. standard 8F Consolidation locomotives. The design and construction as a whole was under the supervision of Mr. R. A. Riddles. No balance is provided for the reciprocating weights, thus following a practice which is growing; e.g., the Southern Railway Merchant Navy Pacifics have no reciprocating balance.

The boiler barrel has a length of 11 ft. 7½ in. and a maximum outside diameter of 5 ft. 8⅛ in. It is parallel, and in this and in the shape of the firebox differs from the Stanier and W.D. locomotives. The length between tubeplates is 12 ft.; the heating surface of the 28 flues 5⅛ in. o.d. is 451 sq. ft., of the 193 tubes of 1¾ in. o.d. 1,061 sq. ft., and of the firebox 168 sq. ft., giving a total evaporative surface of 1,680 sq. ft. The grate area is 28.5 sq. ft., the working pressure 225 lb. per sq. in., and the surface of the 28-element superheater 311 sq. ft. The inside firebox and the side stays in the breaking zone are of copper, but the other stays are of steel. The tubes are of steel and the ashpan of welded steel plate.

Two outside 19 in. by 28 in. cylinders drive the third pair of 56½ in. wheels; the driving wheels are steel castings, but the remaining wheels are of cast iron. The coupled wheels are spread over a base of 16 ft. 3 in., the engine wheelbase is 24 ft. 10 in., the tender wheelbase 15 ft. 9 in., and the engine plus tender wheelbase 53 ft. 1¾ in. Over buffers, engine and tender measure 63 ft. 6 in. The engine weight loaded is 72 tons, of which 62 tons are available for adhesion; but certain locomotives weigh 70.25 tons and have 61.25 tons of adhesion weight. The eight-wheel non-bogie tender weighs 55.5 to 56 tons when loaded with 5,000 gal. of water and 9 tons of coal. Empty weights are 65 tons for the engine and 24½ tons for the tender. A tractive effort of 30,250 lb. is exerted on the basis of 75 per cent. of the boiler pressure. A steam brake is fitted to the locomotive, and Westinghouse and vacuum equipment for train working.

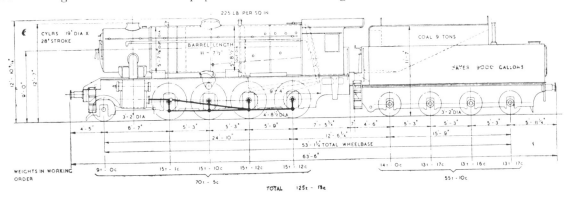

2-10-0 M. OF SUPPLY LOCOMOTIVE

AN event of 1944 was the appearance on British lines of numerous 2-10-0 freight locomotives—the first ten-coupled engines to work anywhere in these islands except on the Lickey incline and on the ex-Great Eastern London suburban routes. These new locomotives were designed under the auspices of the Ministry of Supply for use abroad, but all of them hitherto have been well run-in on British lines, and a sight of them at work was not uncommon. The principal object of the new design was to reduce the maximum axle load of the preceding 2-8-0 design (see page 60) from the very moderate figure of $15\frac{3}{4}$ tons to the low value of $13\frac{1}{2}$ tons; and thus to provide an engine which might be used on light, and even on improvised, tracks. As such lines usually are by no means straight, the 2-10-0 locomotive has the centre pair of wheels flangeless, and the pairs on each side have thin flanges. Leading and trailing coupled axles have a sideplay of $\frac{1}{2}$ in., and all the intermediate axles $\frac{1}{4}$ in.

Compared with the earlier 2-8-0 design a notable modification is the provision of a wide firebox of steel, having a grate area of 40 sq. ft. and a heating surface of 178 sq. ft. inclusive of the 2 ft. combustion chamber, but exclusive of the 14 sq. ft. given by the three 3 in. arch tubes. The barrel contains 152 tubes of $1\frac{7}{8}$ in. o.d. and 28 flues of $5\frac{1}{8}$ in. o.d., 15 ft. 8 in. long, and giving heating surfaces of 1,170 and 589 sq. ft. respectively. The total evaporative surface is 1,951 sq. ft., and the surface of the superheater is 423 sq. ft. Two Ross pop safety valves limit the working pressure to 225 lb. per sq. in. The firebox is arranged for easy conversion to oil firing, but when coal firing is used the grate is in two rocking portions, left hand and right hand. The boiler is lagged with asbestos mattresses and the throat plate with plastic magnesia, whereas the boiler of the standard 2-8-0 had only an air space between the barrel and cleading plates.

Walschaerts valve gear is used to drive the 10 in. piston valves; it provides a maximum travel of $6\frac{5}{8}$ in. and a full-gear cut-off of 75 per cent. Steam lap is $1\frac{1}{2}$ in., exhaust clearance $\frac{1}{16}$ in., lead $\frac{1}{4}$ in., and maximum port opening $1\frac{13}{16}$ in. The 19 in. by 28 in. cylinders drive the third pair of $56\frac{1}{2}$ in. wheels, and at 75 per cent. of the working pressure the tractive effort is 30,200 lb., giving an adhesive factor of 4.96 against the 67.15 tons on the coupled wheels. Both vacuum and Westinghouse air brakes are incorporated for train application, but the locomotive has a steam brake. No brake blocks are fitted to the trailing coupled wheels. Steam sanding gear is provided ahead of the leading coupled wheels and to both sides of the driving wheels.

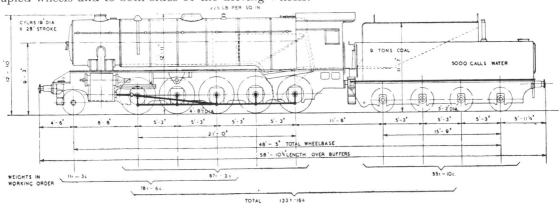

CONTENTS.